SPIRITUAL DIARY

Selected Sayings and Examples of Saints

St. Paul Books & Media

IMPRIMATUR:

Richard Cardinal Cushing

Library of Congress Catalog Card Number: 62-18504

Second Edition, 1990

Copyright, © 1990, 1962 by the Daughters of St. Paul

Printed and published in the U.S.A. by St Paul Books & Media
50 St. Paul's Avenue, Boston, MA 02130

St. Paul Books & Media is the publishing house of the Daughters of St. Paul, an international congregation of women religious serving the Church with the communications media.

4 5 6 7 8 9 10   97 96 95 94 93

FOREWORD

Undoubtedly the *Spiritual Diary* is one of the most widely read works in ascetical literature. From its pages whole generations have drawn their spiritual formation. Even today it is an integral part of many ascetical libraries and its collection of sayings and examples of Saints provides a source of meditation for numerous devout souls.

Countless suppositions have been made as to who is the author of the *Spiritual Diary*. However not one is strong enough to be conclusive. The majority hold that the writer must have been a follower of the school of St. Alphonsus de Liguori (1696-1787), if not one of his intimate companions. Such a conclusion is reached by a study of the volume itself which in its manner of treating virtues one by one appears to be a summary of the various works of St. Alphonsus. Moreover many sayings, considerations and examples have been drawn word for word from his writings.

In the preparation of this new edition of the *Spiritual Diary* the original has been followed as closely as possible. Changes have been made only where necessary to make the content suitable to the modern mentality. It is felt that this will not cause the volume to lose its original freshness but rather will result in an even wider circulation of this priceless collection.

Spiritual Diary treats of twelve virtues, one for each month of the year: *Perfection, Humility, Mortification, Patience, Meekness, Obedience, Simplicity, Diligence, Prayer, Confidence, Charity* and *Union*. Under each virtue are gathered pertinent sayings and examples of Saints for each day. A thought may be read daily or the reader may prefer to read the different sections according to his spiritual needs.

INTRODUCTION

TO THE FOURTH EDITION (1778)

Once again we present you with a new edition of the Spiritual Diary, which made its first appearance three years ago (1775). This is an exact duplicate of the first edition, that is, a collection of sayings and examples of Saints and other souls of deep piety whose lives reflect the spirit and virtues of the Gospels.

Throughout this volume the examples and authority of certain Saints are repeatedly cited: St. Francis de Sales, St. Vincent de Paul, St. Teresa of Avila, St. Mary Magdalene di Pazzi, and others. The author professed a tender devotion to these Saints. He considered them the masters of that real and solid piety and devotion which all souls can and must reflect in their daily lives. Moreover, the path they trod toward perfection is so down-to-earth and practical that no one can reasonably excuse himself from following in their footsteps.

To draw the utmost profit from this volume, mere reading will not suffice. It must be read with calm reflection, deep thought, and ardent desire to translate into action whatever is found to be beneficial to the individual soul.

CONTENTS

January
PERFECTION 9

February
HUMILITY 35

March
MORTIFICATION 55

April
PATIENCE 77

May
MEEKNESS 99

June
OBEDIENCE 126

July
SIMPLICITY 142

August
DILIGENCE 163

September
PRAYER 184

October
CONFIDENCE 204

November
CHARITY 224

December
UNION 245

JANUARY

Perfection

You therefore are to be perfect as your heavenly Father is perfect. Matt. 5:48

1. Act as though all the past were nothing and with David say: "Now I will begin to love my God."
St. Francis de Sales

Thus did St. Paul. Even though after his conversion he had become the Vessel of Election and was filled with the Holy Spirit, he used this method in order to keep on the road to perfection and advance. When writing to the Philippians he said: "Brethren, I do not consider that I have laid hold of it (perfection) already. But one thing I do: forgetting what is behind, I strain forward to what is before, I press on toward the goal to the prize of God's heavenly call in Christ Jesus."

And among the saints who thus counseled and practiced it themselves, we find St. George, St. Bernard and St. Charles. In order to render the necessity and usefulness of this method clear, these saints used two beautiful comparisons. "We should act as do travelers," they said. "They do not look back to see how much they have traveled, but ahead—at the distance they must still cover. This goal they keep before their eyes until the end of the day. Again, we should be like misers who, greedy for riches, do not consider what they have already amassed, nor the fatigue they have endured, but try their utmost to acquire more and multiply their riches daily, as though they had never acquired anything in the past."

✠

2. We must begin with a strong and constant resolution to give ourselves entirely to God, protesting with a tender and loving sentiment, which comes from the depths of the heart, that for the future we want to be His without reserve, and then frequently renew this resolution. *St. Francis de Sales*

Every once in a while, St. Francis de Sales would renew this resolution and his desires to serve God better.

From the first day of his entrance into religious life, St. John Berchmans resolved to become a saint. Not only did he remain constant in all he resolved to do, but also renewed his fervor daily, to his spiritual advantage.

✠

3. God greatly desires us to be so perfect as to be one with Him. Let us examine ourselves and see what is still lacking in us to reach this goal.
St. Teresa of Avila

When Father Peter Fabro, a companion of St. Ignatius, thought of the fact that God greatly desires our perfection, he would try his best to increase in it daily and never let a day pass without some progress in the acquisition of virtue. Thus he grew in perfection and was highly esteemed as a saint.

✠

4. I hear speak of nothing but perfection, but I see it practiced by just a few. Each pictures perfection in his own way. Some see it in simplicity of dress, some in austerity, some in almsgiving, some in the frequenting of the Sacraments; others see it in prayers, others in passive contemplation, and still others in those freely-given or gratuitous graces—but they all err, taking the effects for the cause and the means for the end. I, for my part, know of no other perfection than that of loving God with one's whole heart and one's neighbor as oneself. He who conceives any other type of perfection deceives himself, because the accumulation of all the other virtues without this love is nothing but the amassing of stones. And if we do not immediately and perfectly enjoy this treasure of holy love, it is our own fault, because we are too parsimonious and hesitant with God, and we do not give ourselves entirely to Him as did the Saints.

St. Francis de Sales

From this holy thought, who does not realize that St. Francis de Sales' perfection could not help but be real and very sublime, when his love of God and neighbor was so holy and so pure? The same can be said of St. Vincent de Paul.

St. Mary Magdalene de Pazzi was truly admirable in these two virtues. She acquired such a great love of God and of neighbor that she labored more for the latter's good than for her own.

✠

5. All perfection is based upon two principles, which, if we practice, and attend to the daily duties of our vocation, will surely bring us to its summit and fulfillment. The first principle is a very low opinion of all creation, but above all, of oneself. From this lowly opinion of self will follow the renunciation of oneself and of the things created as well as detachment from self-love, with a resolute will to do one's duty whenever and however necessary. The second principle is a very high esteem of God, which is easily acquired with the light of faith: reflecting that He is omnipotent, the greatest good, our end and has loved us so much. He is always present, He governs us in all, both in nature and in grace and calls each of us to a high perfection, giving us our start with our special vocation. From esteem for God should follow promptness and great submission of the will to all that God wants of us, and at the same time, a complete conformity to the divine Will, which should be the practical gauge of all our plans, affections and deeds. *P. Achille Gagliardi*

Perfection

St. Vincent de Paul's principal concern was to be well established and perfected in these above-mentioned principles. In his profound humility he believed himself utterly incapable of great things, and he thought of nothing else but faithfully fulfilling the obligations a true and perfect Christian has toward God. Then, because he understood through a supernatural light that all Christian perfection depends on the good use of these two principles, he made them his goal and tried his best to engrave them in his soul, so as to make them serve him as a sure rule and guide for every action. And he succeeded in doing so very well, because God, Who exalts the humble, was not only content to lead him, through this means, to that Christian perfection which he was striving to achieve, but also willed to raise him to a solid, eminent and singular sanctity.

✠

6. Perfection consists in one thing only: doing the Will of God. If Our Lord said that in order to be perfect it is enough to deny oneself, take up one's cross and follow Him, who denies himself more, better carries his cross and follows Christ more closely than he who tries his best never to do his own will but always that of God? Now, do you see how little it takes to become a saint? All that is necessary is acquiring the habit of wanting to do the will of God at all times.   *St. Vincent de Paul*

Our Lord said of David that he was a man according to His Heart. And what was the secret of this great sanctity? "Because," He said, "he will do My will in everything."

St. Mary Magdalene de Pazzi was so attached to this, that frequently she would say that she would not do anything, not even the most insignificant thing as, for example, to go from one room to another, if she knew it to be contrary to the will of God; neither would she ever stop doing anything which she believed to be the will of God for her. And if she were to begin something and in the midst of doing it think it to be contrary to God's will, in that very instant she would stop it, even if it should cost her her life.

☩

7. To be a servant of God means to have a great charity toward one's neighbor and an unshakable resolution to follow the divine Will in all things, trusting in God with simplicity and humility, bearing with one's defects and patiently tolerating the imperfections of others. *St. Francis de Sales*

One day, while St. Gertrude was bemoaning the fact that every once in a while she still committed a certain small defect, she begged Our Lord to liberate her from it. He, however, answered her: "Would you then deprive Me of a great honor and yourself of a great reward? Know you, that as often as one recognizes his weakness and resolves to overcome it in the future, he gains a great reward for himself. And each time he refrains from falling for love of Me, he gives Me as great an honor as a good soldier gives to his king when he fights and overcomes his enemies."

✠

8. To be perfect in one's vocation entails nothing else than doing the duties and tasks that one must perform according to his position, but doing them well and only for the love and honor of God, referring all the glory to Him. He who does this is perfect in his state of life; he is a man according to God's Heart and Will. *St. Francis de Sales*

We read in the lives of the holy Fathers that the Abbot Pafnuzio, well known for his sanctity, one day desired to know whether he had any merits before God. In answer he was told that his merits were similar to those of a certain Baron. The saint went to visit that Baron, who received the abbot with kindness and treated him well. After supper, the abbot asked the Baron to tell him of his way of life. The Baron, however, said that he did not have any virtues, but when the abbot insisted, he said that he was most careful to accommodate all travellers and give them what they needed for their journey; he never mistreated the poor, but helped them in their needs; he saw to it that all in his jurisdiction were always treated with justice and that no one could ever complain of having been hurt by his family; he had never saddened anyone, but honored all, helped all those he could and tried his best to keep peace among all. Upon hearing this, the abbot understood that true perfection consists not in doing many things, but in fulfilling one's duties well.

✠

9. Although to one who has entered religion and guards himself against offending God, it might seem that he has done everything, oh! there yet remain certain worms that are not seen until they have eaten away the virtues! These worms are self-love, high esteem of self, rash judgment of others, and lack of charity toward our neighbor. So that, although we fulfill our duties, we do not perform them with that perfection which God wants of us.

St. Teresa of Avila

It was to one of these worms, that the Venerable de Palafox attributed the cause of his falling into mediocrity after his conversion, so much so, that he almost went to the point of losing his soul. "Why," he asked, "should I have thought myself really humble, even though I might be? And even though I tried to be and ardently desired to be good, was I to presume that I really was good? That hidden pride obliged Divine Goodness to teach me to see myself as I really was, not good but bad, lazy, unfaithful, miserable, full of pride and sensuality, and a squanderer of graces."

✠

10. Perfection is not acquired by holding one's arms extended in the form of a cross, but rather by one really working in order to dominate oneself and force oneself to live not according to one's in-

clinations and passions, but according to reason, the Rule and obedience. This is hard, it is true, but it is necessary. With practice, however, it becomes easy and pleasant. *St. Francis de Sales*

Plutarch once related that a certain Lycurgus took two puppies of the same parents and raised one as a house dog and one as a hunting dog. Then, when the dogs were grown, he took them to the forum, where he was to give a talk. First he threw some bones on the ground and at the same time set loose a hare. Upon seeing the bones, the first dog began to chew on them hungrily while the second dog took off to chase the hare. Then Lycurgus called the people's attention, saying: "Did you see what happened? These two dogs are of the same pedigree, yet they do not have the same inclinations; each is inclined to do that which he is accustomed to do." One is able to overcome even the strongest inclinations of nature if one becomes accustomed to self-abnegation.

Of St. Ignatius Loyola, it is written that with the continued self-denial he inflicted upon himself and in his bearing all adversities, he acquired such a degree of holy indifference that it seemed as though he no longer had any inclinations. The same was true of many other saints.

✠

11. All the science of the saints may be reduced to two things: to work and to suffer. He who best does these two things, becomes a greater saint.
St. Francis de Sales

We find in the lives of the holy Fathers of the Church, that St. Dorotheus thus led his disciple, St. Dositheus, in the work of his sanctification. He kept his disciple constantly busy, especially in those things contrary to his will. Hence, if St. Dorotheus saw him with something in his hands, even though necessary for what he was doing, such as a knife, book or other similar objects, he would immediately take it from him. If he asked news about something, even about something good, he was sent away without a reply. Thus, in all his desires, St. Dorotheus sought to deny him and St. Dositheus promptly obeyed in all things and suffered all in silence. In this way he reached a high degree of perfection within the short period of five years.

✠

12. I would like to persuade spiritual persons that the way to perfection does not consist of many methods nor much thinking, but in denying oneself in everything and suffering everything for the love of Jesus Christ. If this exercise is lacking, all the other modes of walking in the spiritual way lead astray, even though the person should have reached a high degree of contemplation and communication with God. *St. John of the Cross*

One day Blessed Angela of Foligno had an ecstasy during which she saw Our Lord caressing some of His servants, but some He caressed more than others. Desiring to know the reason for this diversity of treatment, she asked Our Lord and He answered: "I call all to Me, but

Perfection

not everyone wishes to come, because the way is covered with thorns. Those who do follow Me, I invite to My table and to drink of My cup. But because My foods are distasteful to the senses and My chalice is full of bitterness, not everyone cares to satiate himself with those things with which I nourished Myself while on earth. Of course, those who are most faithful to Me are dearest to Me and are My favorites." Upon hearing this, Blessed Angela was filled with such an ardent desire for suffering and self-denial that upon encountering great difficulties she enjoyed as much consolation as a worldly person would enjoy in his favorite pastime.

✠

13. The worst thing that can befall persons who have good will is to want to be what they cannot be and not want to be what they necessarily must be. They conceive desires to do great things, which perhaps will never be expected of them; in the meantime, they neglect the little things which God puts into their hands. There are thousands of acts of virtue as, for example, to bear little troubles and the imperfections of our neighbors; to suffer a biting word or some little injustice; to repress a harsh word; to mortify a little attachment or curiosity; to refrain from giving a bit of news; to excuse an indiscretion; to be condescending toward others in little things—these are for everyone, so why not practice them? Very seldom do we have the opportunity to gain large "sums", but we can

daily earn little ones. And with the intelligent handling of these little "earnings", there are many who become rich. Oh, how many merits we would earn and what great saints we would become if we were to take advantage of every occasion that our vocation offers us! *St. Francis de Sales*

Inflamed with the great desire of martyrdom, St. Philip Neri resolved to go to preach the Faith in India. But upon learning, through a revelation, that God wished his India to be in Rome, there he remained and led such a virtuous life that he became a great saint.

In just five years of religious life, St. John Berchmans attained a high degree of perfection. What did he do? Nothing exceptional. He did his best to be faithful and exact in all his duties, never neglecting any means which, with the help of grace, could help him to acquire this perfection.

In the life of a young Jesuit seminarian we read that one morning when he was about to go out for a game with his companions, a Priest asked him to give up the game and go to serve his Mass. The seminarian did so. Years later, when that seminarian was ordained, he went to preach the Faith to the infidels and had the grace of dying a martyr. Then it was revealed that it was because of that mortification of not going out to play with the others but of remaining in to serve Mass, that he received such a great reward.

Perfection

✠

14. The trouble with us is that we want to serve God in our own way and not in His, and according to our own will, not His. When He permits that we be ill, we want to be well; when He wills that we serve Him in sufferings, we desire to serve Him with works; when He wants us to exercise charity, we want to exercise humility; when He wants resignation from us, we want devotion, piety or some other virtue. And this, not because the things we want are more pleasing to Him, but because they give us greater satisfaction. This, undoubtedly, is the greatest impediment to our perfection, because if we want to become saints according to our will we will never become saints. In order really to become a saint it is best to do so according to God's will. *St. Francis de Sales*

St. Mary Magdalene well understood the great importance of this truth. With it as a sure guide, she submitted her will to that of God in such a manner that she was always happy, no matter what happened. She never desired anything contrary to the will of God. To ask God any graces for herself or for others with insistence was deemed by her a great defect; she said it was better to ask for graces with simple prayers and that she gloried and took pleasure in doing God's will rather than her own. Furthermore, she even desired to acquire the degree of sanctity God wanted of her rather than the degree she might want. Hence she wrote this resolution: "I will to offer myself to God, to want all and only that perfection which

He wishes me to acquire and in the way and time He wishes and in no other way." Once, while confiding to one of her Sisters she said: "The good that does not come to me by way of the will of God, does not seem good, and I would prefer not to have any gift but that of leaving all my will and desires in God, rather than to have a gift which I desire or will."

☩

15. I see two common mistakes among spiritual persons. The first is that they measure their devotions by the consolations and satisfactions that they experience in the service of God; so much so, that if these are lacking at times, they feel that they have lost all their piety. No, this is nothing but a sensible devotion. The true and substantial devotion does not consist in these things, but in having a will that is resolute, active, prompt and constant in not offending God and in fulfilling all that which appertains to His service. The second mistake is that if they should ever do something with repugnance or weariness, they feel that they have not gained any merit. On the contrary they have gained greater merit, for a single ounce of good performed with weariness and without satisfaction while the soul is undergoing a period of spiritual darkness, is worth more than one hundred pounds of good done with pleasure and satisfaction, be-

cause the first was performed with a stronger and purer love than the latter. Hence, no matter how much aridity and repugnance the sensitive part of us may feel, we must not lose courage but continue along our way.   *St. Francis de Sales*

In order to prevent his penitents from falling into the first mistake, St. Philip Neri used to tell them that in the spiritual life there are three degrees or stages. The first is called animal life and is of those who in their devotions seek sensible consolations. These consolations are given by God to beginners so that, attracted by the delight derived from the sensible pleasure, they will give themselves to the spiritual life. The second is called the life of man, and is of those who, deprived of sensible sweetness, combat their passions for the acquisition of virtue. The third is called life of the angels. This life is reached by those who, having fought for a long time to overcome their passions, receive from God a tranquil, quiet and almost angelic life even in this world.

✠

16. It is not as necessary to strive for great favors as it is to gain virtue, for the one who makes mortifications and, with humility and purity of conscience, serves the Lord is the one who, without doubt, will be the greatest saint.
St. Teresa of Avila

Rufino d'Aquileia narrates that one day, while praying, St. Macarius, who thought he had progressed quite well in virtue, heard an interior voice say: "Macarius, know that you have not yet reached the virtue which is found in those two women who live in that city." Macarius went to visit those two women. After questioning and examining them, he found them to be quite advanced in virtue; for, although they had lived together for fifteen years, they had never disagreed either in words or in actions. Surprised, St. Macarius confessed that those two women were holier than he, even though he had received so many and such extraordinary graces.

✠

17. Lord, what wilt Thou have me do? Behold the true sign of a totally perfect soul: when one has reached the point of giving up his will so completely that he no longer seeks, expects or desires to do ought but that which God wills.

St. Bernard

These were St. Paul's first words as soon as he came to know Jesus: "Lord, what wilt Thou have me do?" He said these words with such sincere affection and such submission of his will, that from then on he had no other desire than to fulfill the divine will. Neither did he ever vacillate in his constancy and fidelity, regardless of how many adversities, sufferings or trials he encountered.

✠

18. If you really want to become perfect, you must firmly hold to the counsel of the Apostle:

Perfection

Attend to yourself, which implies two things. The first is not to look at the affairs of others nor at their defects. For the one who wishes to do his duty well and correct his own faults certainly has enough to do. The second is to strive for your own perfection and work incessantly for it, without worrying whether or not the others are doing so.

Abbot Pastore

St. John Berchmans was an outstanding example in this regard. From the first day of his religious life, St. John Berchmans resolved that he would tend only and always to his own affairs. To this he dedicated all his life with such solicitude, that he never had time to look at the affairs of the others or to notice their defects. Hence he never stopped to reflect why others did or said this or that, or whether they acted well or not. Nor did he ever take it upon himself to defend one at the risk of offending others. He just quietly let each one think of himself and take care of his own affairs. As for the defects of the others, he took no notice of them even when committed before his eyes. For this reason it can be said that he never was able to point out the defects in the others. All he worried about was to correct his defects and to do his duties well. Therefore, in order to keep his soul free from defects, he used extraordinary diligence. Although he had a great love for studies, he never let his studies interfere with his spiritual exercises, acts of charity or obedience; he never sought to satisfy his desires but to gain as many merits as possible.

✠

19. Never let pass a single occasion of merit from which you can gain some spiritual profit as, for example, some harsh little word someone might say, an obedience asked of you against your will, a chance to humiliate yourself, to practice charity, meekness and patience. All these occasions are profitable to you and you yourself should look for them. And you should go to sleep quite content on the day that you have had more occasions of merit, just as the businessman does when he has had the opportunity of realizing a profit, for on that day business went well for him. *St. Ignatius*

As we read in the life of St. John Berchmans, this was one of his principal maxims. He did his utmost not to let slip any occasion of merit for himself, no matter how small. Hence he went about seeking such occasions, and when some came through someone's indiscretion, he embraced them all with courage and joy of heart, without considering the indiscretion and little virtue of the others, but solely attending to his own humility.

✠

20. Set yourselves seriously to work for the acquisition of virtue; otherwise your spiritual growth will be stunted. Neither should you think that you have acquired a virtue if you have not

been tried by its opposite and have not had the occasion to faithfully practice it. Therefore, you should never flee the occasions to practice it, but rather desire them, seek them and willingly embrace them.
St. Teresa of Avila

St. Vincent de Paul was not satisfied, as many are, to know and love virtues; he tried his best to exercise them. His maxim was that fatigue and patience are the best means to acquire virtues and plant them in our heart, because the virtues acquired without fatigue and trials also can be lost easily, while those acquired by combatting storms of temptations and practiced in spite of difficulties and repugnance of nature will take deep roots in one's heart.

✠

21. Humility and charity are the two main parts of the spiritual edifice. One is the lowest and the other the highest and all the others depend on them. Hence, we must keep ourselves well founded in these two, because the preservation of the entire edifice depends on the foundation and the roof.
St. Francis de Sales

There never was and there never will be a saint without these two very necessary virtues; in fact, there have been some who, to our eyes, seem to have excelled in these virtues in a special way. One of these was St. Francis of Paula who, for his great humility, not content to be looked upon as the least among all men, willed that his Religious Congregation be given that same title.

✠

22. The two feet with which one walks towards perfection are mortification and the love of God. The first is the left foot, the latter is the right.

St. Francis of Assisi rose to great heights of perfection with these two means. He led such an austere and rigorous life that when he was dying he had to apologize to his body for mistreating it so much. Because of his love of God, he acquired not only for himself but also for his Order the beautiful title of "seraphic".

When St. Francis de Sales wanted to prepare someone to live a truly Christian life and to abandon his worldly ways, he seldom spoke of exterior things, such as the hair, dress or some such thing. Rather, he spoke only to the heart and of the heart. He knew that once this fortress is overcome, all the rest will surrender and that when true love of God takes possession of the heart, all those things which are not of God will lose importance.

✠

23. When one is truly advancing towards perfection, he feels within himself a constant urge to progress and improve. Because the more grace of enlightenment he receives, the more he realizes how much he is still lacking in virtue and good works. On the other hand, if he does realize that he is doing a little good, he feels it is very imper-

Perfection

fect and does not give it much credit. Hence he continuously works for perfection without slacking in pace. *St. Lawrence Justinian*

St. Fulgentius loved perfection so much that no matter how much he worked for it, it always seemed so little and always he desired to be more perfect.

Daily St. Ignatius would compare his victories with those of the previous day, and thus he advanced daily, always with a greater desire for progress so as to reach the height of perfection which Our Lord desired of him.

St. James the Apostle is highly praised because daily he advanced in the service of God.

☩

24. A true sign that one loves the virtue he is striving to acquire is to appreciate the corrections and admonitions received for the defects committed against this virtue. This is a great indication of advancing toward perfection. *St. Francis de Sales*

Once a monk went to visit the Abbot Serapione. The abbot requested that before doing anything else they pray together; but the monk refused, stating that he was a sinner and unworthy to wear the habit. Whereupon, the abbot said: "My brother, if you wish to become perfect remain in your cell to work and do not talk too much, for to go about here and there is not good for you." At these words the monk became greatly disturbed. Seeing this, the abbot added: "What is this, my brother? Until now you said you were a great sinner and not worthy to be alive. And now because I admonished you with charity, telling you what you needed, you become indignant? It seems to me that your humility is not real. If you really want to be humble, learn to receive admonitions humbly." At these words, the monk repented and left, greatly edified.

When St. Peter was corrected by St. Paul, he did not become indignant nor angry because he was superior to St. Paul; neither did he despise Paul because he had been a persecutor of the Church. He took the correction well.

It is related that whenever St. Ambrose would receive a correction for some fault, he would thank the person correcting him as though he had received a great benefit. We are told that whenever a certain Cistercian monk received a correction, he would recite an *Our Father* for the admonisher.

St. John Berchmans always desired to be corrected in public for his defects, and whenever this happened, he was very happy.

✠

25. The greatest guarantee that we can have of being in the state of grace does not consist in feelings and sentiments of love of God, but in the pure and irrevocable abandonment of our entire being into God's hands and in the firm resolution never to consent to sin, whether grievous or slight.
St. Francis de Sales

Perfection

St. Catherine of Genoa used to say: "I am no longer my own; whether I live or I die, I belong to my Savior. I have nothing which is my very own. My God is my all. My life is entirely His. O world, you are always the same and until now I have been the same, but from now on I will change."

✠

26. By contemplating Baby Jesus in the manger, let us learn how to esteem the things of the world. *St. Francis de Sales*

When St. Hedwig, Queen of Poland, became a religious, she never spoke of the things of the world unless it was for the honor of God and the salvation of souls.

✠

27. If you want a brief and efficacious method, which at the same time embraces all the other methods, to overcome any temptations and trials, and to acquire perfection, it is living in the presence of God. *St. Basil*

When Joseph was being tempted to commit sin he asked: "How can I do this in the presence of God?" And Susanna said to the wicked judges: "It is better I fall into your hands innocent than to commit sin in the sight of God."

Taide, upon learning that when she sinned she was seen by God, was converted. She remained firm in the face of many temptations, thus becoming a saint.

28. In order to make great strides toward perfection, it is wise to attach oneself to only one thing: one spiritual book, one virtue, one aspiration and so forth. It is not that the other means should be rejected, but the one that has been chosen should be the principal object of attention, so that even if one needs to be attentive to other spiritual exercises these will be only secondary. However, there is one defect into which many fall, and it must be avoided. It is the defect of attaching oneself to one's practices of piety and devotions too strongly. He who has a good spirit is edified by all things and condemns nothing.

St. Francis de Sales

Although the saints availed themselves of everything, each one had a particular practice in which he exercised himself the most. Thus St. Francis de Sales' most favorite book was Scupoli's "Spiritual Combat"; St. Dominic's was Cassiano's "Collection"; the aspiration preferred by St. Francis was: "My God is my all"; that of St. Vincent de Paul: "In the name of God." Some stressed the practice of living in God's presence; others, purity of intention; others, submission to the divine Will; still others, self-abnegation. The same may be said about virtues. Some exercised one, others another virtue. Thus almost every saint rendered himself outstanding in one virtue in particular.

✠

29. If you wish to reach quickly the summit of perfection, truly love humiliations, insults and calumnies. *St. Ignatius*

It is narrated of St. Catherine of Bologna, that whenever she received an insult or contempt she felt great joy and her love of humiliation increased. Thus she grew so much in her love of God that in order to do His will she was ready, she once stated, not only to suffer all the torments of the world, but also all those of hell.

✠

30. Place yourself under the discipline of a severe and austere man, one who treats you harshly and with rigor, and then do your utmost to drink in those reprehensions and harsh treatment as though you were enjoying milk and honey. I assure you that within a short time you will have reached the peak of perfection. *Abbot Moses*

The monk, John Tebeo, as we are told in the lives of the Fathers, served one of the old, sick priests for twelve years, with diligence and love. Although that priest saw how hard and burdensome that duty was for the monk, he never said a kind or loving word to him, but treated him harshly. When however, he was dying, the priest called to the monk, took him by the hand and said to him three times: "Be with God." Then he recommended the monk to the other priests, saying: "He is not a man, but an Angel!"

✠

31. Certain that the doctrine of Christ cannot deceive us, we must, in order to walk securely, trustingly hold to His doctrine and resolve to act always according to its maxims rather than to those of the world, which are fallacious. This is the fundamental maxim of all Christian perfection.
St. Vincent de Paul

Frequently St. Francis de Sales was saddened by his friends because they did not approve of his ways. They wanted him to defend himself more vigorously against the calumnies of the wicked and to maintain his dignity. He, however, would answer that meekness should be the characteristic of bishops. Hence, even though the world and self-love had established other maxims, he would not avail himself of these, because they were contrary to those of Jesus Christ.

FEBRUARY

Humility

> *For everyone who exalts himself shall be humbled, and he who humbles himself shall be exalted.* Luke 14:11

1. Humility is the foundation of all the other virtues; hence, in the soul in which this virtue does not exist there cannot be any other virtue except in mere appearance. Similarly, it is the best disposition to receive celestial gifts. Finally, it is so necessary for perfection that, among all the ways to reach it, the first is humility, the second is humility, and the third is humility. And if I were asked about it one hundred times, I would still give the same answer.

St. Augustine

St. Louis Gonzaga was well aware of this truth. His one aim was to gain the virtue of humility. For this reason, each day he recited a particular prayer to the Angels so that they would help him walk along this straight path, which they themselves had first traveled, and hence be able to occupy the place of one of them who had fallen because of pride.

✠

2. Humility is the mother of many virtues because from it obedience, fear, reverence, patience, modesty, meekness and peace are born. He

who is humble easily obeys everyone, fears to offend everyone, is at peace with everyone, is kind with all, is submissive to everyone, does not offend or displease anyone, does not resent the injuries inflicted upon him; he lives happy, contented and in great peace. *St. Thomas of Villanova*

St. Jane Frances de Chantal had such a great love for this virtue, that she always was on guard never to let slip by an occasion of humiliation, no matter how small.

✠

3. He who is not very humble can never make progress in contemplation; for this reason any small action performed with pride, even though it may seem nothing, is of great harm. *St. Teresa of Avila*

Because Blessed Clare of Montefalco took pride in one of her works, Our Lord deprived her of His celestial consolations for fifteen years. And no matter what she did to reacquire them, whether she shed many tears, did penance, or scourged herself, she could not receive them during that period of time.

✠

4. Humility is necessary not only for the acquisition of virtues, but also for our salvation because, as Jesus said, the door of heaven is narrow and only the little ones can enter. *St. Bernard*

Humility

The Pharisee was separated from the rest of the people because his profession was a type of religion in which he prayed, fasted and performed many other good deeds. Nevertheless, he was deemed blameworthy by God. Why? Because he lacked humility. He took pride in his good works and gloried in them as though he had performed them by his own power.

✠

5. The most powerful weapon with which to overcome the devil is humility; because, not knowing how to use it, he does not even know how to defend himself from it. *St. Vincent de Paul*

One day, while St. Macarius was returning to his cell he met the devil who tried to cut him in half with a sickle. He could not do so, because when he drew near the saint he lost his energy. Then, full of anger he said: "I suffer great violence from you, Macarius, because though I greatly desire to harm you, I cannot. I do all that you do and more. You fast once in a while, I never eat. You sleep little, I never close my eyes. You are chaste, and so am I. In one thing only do you surpass me." "And what is this thing?" asked Macarius. He answered: "It is your great humility." And with that he disappeared!

✠

6. Humble persons, those who humble themselves and seek to be despised by the others,

are highly pleasing to God. He willingly lowers himself to them, and pours down the treasures of His graces upon them; to them He reveals His secrets; He calls them and draws them to Himself. The more one lowers himself in the eyes of men, the higher he ascends, the greater he becomes in the eyes of God and the more clearly he will one day see the Divine Essence. *Thomas a Kempis*

St. Bonaventure used to say: "I know what to do to placate God. I will consider myself as dung, I will render myself intolerable to myself; and when I shall see myself humiliated and scorned, trampled upon and filled with ignominies, I shall rejoice and be happy. I will ask help from all the creatures of God, desiring to be confounded and punished by them, since I offended their Creator."

Not only did St. Francis of Assisi repute himself nothing, the greatest sinner in the world and worthy of hell, but also unworthy of God's thought of him. While he was saying these things to one of his companions one day, the latter saw in a vision that a place was prepared for Francis among the seraphim.

✠

7. A day of humble recognition of self, although there may have been many afflictions and pains, is a greater grace of God than many days of prayer. *St. Teresa of Avila*

The venerable Mother Seraphina of God once had a revelation in which she clearly saw and understood that God, being the purest truth, cannot see in Himself anything except infinite perfections which He enjoys and takes pleasure in. When God wills to unite a soul to Himself, He gives that soul a light of truth through which she sees, without horror or error, her condition. She sees that by herself she never did anything good, nor is she capable of doing so; that she only has inclinations to do evil, and whatever she may have of good in her comes from God. Standing in this bright light, even though the soul may appear ugly, deformed and hateful to herself, in the eyes of God, however, she is beautiful and pleasing because she has begun to resemble His own true and perfectly clear nature. The same servant of God, after having led an innocent and very perfect life, came to know her imperfections with such clarity that they seemed to her as grave and horrible sins. For these she conceived such a great sorrow that she could not find peace. Hence, when reprimanded for something she had done, she was not in the least agitated, but would say to herself: "What you see is nothing. If you could see everything, oh how you would abhor me and flee from me!" But God consoled her interiorly, telling her that her past imperfections seemed big because her soul was in the state of that bright light; and in reality, those defects were no longer there, since He had washed them away with His blood.

✠

8. Look upon yourself as insignificant; gladly consent to be considered as such by the others; do not become puffed up because of God's gifts to you—and you will be truly humble.

St. Bonaventure

Thus was St. Mary Magdalene de Pazzi. It has been written of her that in her own eyes she appeared so miserable that she continuously regarded herself as the lowest of creatures. And as she appeared to herself, thus always she desired to appear in the eyes of the others. Hence, whenever she was scorned or in some way rejected, such was her great joy for the humiliation, that often she was rapt in ecstasy. She could not suffer to be honored, nor did she want others to esteem her. Therefore frequently, both in public and in private, she would accuse herself of the smallest defect. Moreover, she did her utmost to hide her virtues and good works. When she could not hide them, she made little of them. Because she could not hide or stop her ecstasies, she felt very bad to be seen and heard, and one day complained to Our Lord: "Oh, my Jesus, why have You had so many things pass between You and me alone and now You want me to make them known? Did You not promise that just as You were hidden, so must I be?"

☩

9. Humility, which Jesus recommended both with words and examples, must have the following three conditions: first, we must sincerely esteem ourselves worthy of all insults from our fellowmen; second, take pleasure in having others see how imperfect we are and for that reason despise us; third, no matter how much God works in us or through us, if it is at all possible, hide it in view of our nothingness, and when it cannot be concealed, attribute it to the divine mercy and to the merits of others.

St. Vincent de Paul

St. Clare very evidently possessed this first condition, for she was wont to say to her companions: "Oh, Sisters, if you knew me better, you would abhor me, because I am not what you think me to be."

St. Francis Borgia was so immersed in his low concept of himself that he was surprised when people greeted him on the street.

St. Vincent de Paul's humility possessed these three conditions. He had such a low esteem of self that he reputed himself a great sinner, a burden on all and unworthy to be a member of his Congregation. And just as he had a low concept of himself, he desired the same from the others. Hence, he desired everyone to know his imperfections and frequently he would reveal them to all in order to be looked down upon and despised by all. He could not bear praises or honors. One day, a poor woman, thinking that by praising him he would give her more alms, said to a number of distinguished people surrounding him that she had once been his noble mother's servant. But the saint, disliking that praise, immediately said: "My good woman, you deceive yourself. My mother never had a servant; in fact, she herself was a servant." For this same reason, he was never heard to speak of the many great things he did nor of the wonderful things that happened to him.

✠

10. We must consider the others as our superiors always, and subject ourselves to them even though they may be inferior to us, anticipating their desires with respect and submission. O, what a won-

derful thing this would be if God were pleased to establish us in such a practice! *St. Vincent de Paul*

This St. Vincent de Paul practiced very well. He esteemed everyone and held everyone as better than himself. For him, all were more prudent, more perfect, and more capable than he was; hence he had no difficulty in being submissive to the will of the others.

✠

11. Our Lord says that he who wishes to become greater than the others must make himself the least of all. This is a truth which all Christians believe, yet how is it that so few put it into practice?
St. Vincent de Paul

As St. Jerome attests, St. Paula was outstanding for her humility. If anyone who did not know her had seen her, he would have thought her the least of all because, surrounded by pious virgins, she dressed, spoke and walked as though she were the least of all.

✠

12. Do not believe that you have made progress toward perfection if you do not think yourself the least of all and if you do not desire to be neglected by all. What distinguishes those who are great in the eyes of God is to be lowly in their own

eyes and, the more glorious they are in God's eyes, the more vile they appear to themselves.

St. Teresa of Avila

It is related in the lives of the Fathers that a certain monk revealed his interior life to Abbot Sisois and told him that he always carried within himself the thought of God. The abbot answered him: "This is not such a great thing. The great thing would be your considering yourself the least of all creatures."

☩

13. When one is outstanding in virtue, truly great before God and favored by Him and, notwithstanding this, he considers himself small and of no importance, he has that humility which is so pleasing to God and so rare among men. It is that humility found in so perfect a manner in the Blessed Virgin who, upon hearing herself chosen Mother of God, declared herself His handmaid. *St. Bernard*

St. Teresa, thinking of the abundance of graces she received from God, would humiliate herself, saying that God sustained her in her weakness, and that by His divine help showed her how weak she was—just as props against a delapidated house show its weakness.

✠

14. Vain complacency, the desire to be seen, to be the main topic of conversation, to be praised and told we are doing well and performing wonders—this is an evil which leads to the forgetfulness of God and the spoiling of our holiest actions. It is the most pernicious vice in our spiritual life. I cannot understand how one who holds as a truth of faith that he who exalts himself shall be humbled, can seek to be known as a distinguished, wise, prudent and capable person. *St. Vincent de Paul*

It is related that a famous Brother Justin, after refusing great favors and an honorable position offered him by the king of Hungary, became a religious and made such spiritual progress, that frequently he went into ecstasy. One day, while all were at table, he was rapt into ecstasy and, rising above the other religious, went to honor an image of the Blessed Mother, which was painted high up on the wall. Because of this, Pope Eugene IV sent for the Brother and, not permitting him to kiss his foot, embraced him. Then the Pope invited him to sit and together they had a long conversation after which he gave Brother Justin some gifts and granted him many indulgences. The Brother, however, became proud and St. John of Capistrano, upon seeing him, said: "You left us an angel and you have returned a devil!" In fact, from then on he grew in insolence and finally fled to the kingdom of Naples where, because of his many wicked deeds, he died in jail.

Humility

From his infancy, St. Thomas Aquinas always disliked praise and never said a word of praise about himself. Hence he never suffered a temptation of vanity or of complacency, as he himself admitted to Brother Reginald, saying that he thanked God for the grace of never having been tormented by pride.

✠

15. O my God, what do we expect to reap if we seek to appear great in the eyes of men? What does it matter whether we are ridiculed and regarded as insignificant by men, if in Your eyes we are great and without fault? Oh, will we ever understand this truth and thus arrive at the peak of perfection! The saints had but one desire—that of being unknown and regarded as inferior by everyone. *St. Bernard*

The Empress Leonora, upon finding out that her confessor had written about her many heroic acts and virtues in order to diffuse them after her death, went to visit him frequently during his last illness and insisted until he gave her the manuscript. Then, upon returning home, she threw it into the fire.

✠

16. When you see someone who desires honor and esteem, who flees contempt and, when contradicted, is resentful and becomes downcast, rest assured that even though this person might perform

miracles, he is still very far from perfection because all his virtue is without a foundation.

St. Thomas Aquinas

Thus the Angelic Doctor thought and acted. He not only did not desire honors and praises but also fled and abhorred them. When Pope Clement IV offered him the dignity of Archbishop of Naples, at the very time in which his relatives had fallen from the emperor's favor and hence had been reduced to poverty, they tried to induce him to accept the favor. He, however, refused, obtaining from the same Pope the promise of never being raised to any dignity. Moreover, he begged his superiors not to force him to receive the degree of Doctor of Philosophy; it was only because of obedience that he did receive it. On the other hand, he did not flee from derision; rather, he gladly accepted it and always with a tranquil and serene countenance. When a student, he did not disdain to have as private tutor one of his own school-fellows who, seeing that he did not talk much, and thinking that it was because he was stupid, called him "dumb ox". However, he soon thought differently when he saw that St. Thomas could be not only his tutor, but also his master. One day, while reading in the refectory, the saint was corrected for the pronunciation of a word. Even though he knew that he had pronounced it correctly, he immediately repeated it. When asked why he had done so, he answered: "Because it matters little if a syllable is pronounced long or short, but it matters greatly whether one is humble and obedient."

17. I am despised and derided and I am troubled; such is the way peacocks and monkeys act. I am mocked and ridiculed and I rejoice; thus did the Apostles react. This is the deepest degree of humility: to rejoice when one is humiliated and jeered at, just as the vain person takes pride in great honors; and to feel hurt when honored and esteemed, as the proud person suffers when taunted and ridiculed.
St. Francis de Sales

St. Dominic remained more willingly in the diocese of Carcassona than in that of Tolouse, where he had converted many heretics. When asked why, he answered: "Because in the latter there are many honors, while in the former nothing but insults and hard work."

St. Costantius, a Premonstratensian Priest who was in a parish near Ancona, Italy, was so detached from the world that he had gained renown among the people as a man of great virtue. Hence, people came from distant places just to get a glimpse of him. Among these, a farmer, upon seeing the saint standing on a step ladder changing a lamp, and noticing how small and thin the saint was, exclaimed aloud to himself: "I thought he was a great man, but I see he does not even look like one!" Upon hearing this, the saint leaped down from the ladder, ran up to the man and cried as he embraced him: "You alone, among so many, have kept your eyes open and have seen me as I really am."

✠

18. He who is truly humble never thinks that any injustice is made him. We should be ashamed of ourselves when we resent having anything said or done against us. It is a terrible thing to see our Creator bearing such great insults from His creatures while we are so resentful for the least harsh word spoken to us. Nothing bothers the soul that is united to God and she does not worry whether she is esteemed or not; nor if good or bad is said of her; in fact she prefers dishonor and trials to honors and pleasure. *St. Teresa of Avila*

Whenever St. Francis de Sales would notice that those around him were displeased at something unkind said about him or to him, he would say to them, "When did I give you the authority to resent the affronts meant for me? Let them say what they please. This is a cross of words only, the memory of which will perish. One must be quite 'touchy' to resent the annoyance of a fly. Do we pretend to be irreprehensible? Who knows, perhaps they see my faults better than I do and might be the ones who really love me. What harm can they do us by having a lowly opinion of us, when we ourselves should be the ones to have it?"

✠

19. He who is truly humble, when humiliated humiliates himself all the more; when rejected, en-

Humility

joys the scorn; when given a lowly task, considers himself honored more than he deserves and performs it willingly. The only thing he abhors and flees are dignities and high offices.

St. Jane Frances de Chantal

Because of the singularity of St. Rose of Lima's life, she frequently was insulted and rebuked by her mother and brothers. However, the humble girl always believed she deserved worse treatment than that, hence she not only did not excuse herself, but also exaggerated things, so that they would not become aware that she was undeserving of such punishment.

✠

20. To suffer willingly rejection and insult is the touch-stone of humility and true virtue. Following this practice, one is more like Jesus, Who is the true model of every solid virtue.

St. Francis de Sales

We read in the lives of the Fathers, that St. Amonio reached such a high degree of perfection that he was as insensible to injuries as a stone, and no matter how many were inflicted upon him, he never regarded them as such.

✠

21. The truly humble soul must sincerely desire to be despised, derided, persecuted and falsely

accused. How else can he better imitate Jesus Christ? Oh! how wise he will one day be acknowledged who on earth was happy to be regarded as unworthy of the approval and even the good opinion of others! *St. Teresa of Avila*

A Jansenist, finding that he was unable to influence St. Vincent de Paul into accepting his false doctrines, became indignant and heaped him with insults. Among other things he called him an ignoramous and was astonished that his Congregation kept him as Superior General. The Saint answered, "I am surprised myself, for I am more ignorant than you can imagine."

✠

22. If we were to examine well all that which is human and imperfect in us, we would, unfortunately, find enough cause to humiliate ourselves before God and men, even if they should be our inferiors. *St. Vincent de Paul*

The Venerable Mother Seraphina of God enlightened by God saw her soul filled with many defects. However, the Saint was not surprised. In her profound humility she believed it should look worse. As she said, "If I were more illumined, I would see more." Throughout her life nothing ever caused her to change her opinion about herself.

✠

23. In my opinion, we will never acquire true humility if we do not lift up our eyes to God. Contemplating His greatness, the soul clearly sees its own lowliness; considering God's patience, it sees how far it is from being patient. In fact, contemplating the divine perfections, the soul sees its own great imperfections. *St. Teresa of Avila*

This, in fact, was one of the principal fonts from which St. Vincent de Paul derived his low concept of himself and his great desire for humiliations: his knowledge of God's infinite perfections and man's miseries and weaknesses. Hence it seemed to him an evident injustice not to be humble always and in all things. While speaking to his confreres one day he said: "In truth, if each one of us would try to know himself better, he would realize that it is only right to humiliate oneself. If we seriously were to stop to consider our natural inclination to evil, our inability to perform any good, and the experience that, even when we think we have succeeded in doing something well, very often it turns out the opposite and God permits us to be humiliated, would we not be humble ourselves, seeing ourselves so far from sanctity, from the high degree of God's perfection and the stupendous works of His grace?"

✠

24. If one truly wishes to become a saint, he must never excuse himself, with the exception of a

few cases, even though he may be falsely accused. Thus did Jesus act. He was accused of evil of which He was innocent, but He never uttered a word to free Himself of that humiliation. *St. Philip Neri*

St. Vincent de Paul never excused himself, regardless of what he was accused or the calumnies that were spread about him or his Congregation, no matter how much suffering or harm these brought him. Because he used his influence to prevent one of his subjects, whom he judged unworthy, from being made bishop, the latter spread a serious calumny about him. The calumny reached the queen's ears and she, upon seeing the saint, told him he should prove his innocence. Without becoming disturbed in the least, he answered: "Madame, many things were said to Christ and He never excused Himself."

☩

25. Very often one reaches perfection sooner by not excusing himself than by listening to ten sermons. The reason for this is that, by not excusing oneself, one begins to acquire spiritual liberty, and no longer worries about what others think or say about him. In fact, by making it a habit to refrain from answering, one will reach the point of hearing others speak of him and yet feel as though they were not speaking of him. *St. Teresa of Avila*

Father Alvarez, who was St. Teresa of Avila's confessor, was falsely accused of a grave fault. This was done at a

Humility

provincial meeting, and he was severely corrected in public. However, Father Alvarez never excused himself, neither in public nor in private. For this heroic silence, God rewarded him with extraordinary favors.

✠

26. One of the best ways to acquire humility is to fix the following maxim in our mind: One is worth what he is worth in the eyes of God.
Thomas a Kempis

St. Francis de Sales practiced this maxim perfectly. He did not worry about his reputation, and cared not at all of what the others might think of him. To one he once confided: "Oh! If it would only please God never to reveal my innocence, not even at the last judgment, but to keep it eternally hidden in the secrets of His Eternal Wisdom!" Another time he exclaimed: "If the grace of God should have worked some good through me, I would be happy if, on the day of judgment when all the secrets of hearts will be revealed, only God should know my good works and everyone should see my faults, instead."

✠

27. All those who have really wanted to possess humility have given themselves wholeheartedly to the practice of humiliations, because in this they recognized the short cut to the acquisition of the virtue.
St. Bernard

When Blessed Alexander Sauli, Bishop of Aleria, a learned and highly esteemed man, was superior of his Community, he always undertook the menial tasks, such as sweeping, washing dishes, carrying wood, working in the garden, serving the sick, answering the door, ringing the bells, helping the sacristan, and so on. When, because of priestly duties, he was unable to perform those tasks, he would redouble his work the following day.

✠

28. To be genuine, humility must be accompanied by charity, that is, we must love, seek and accept humiliations so as to please God and resemble Jesus. Otherwise, we would be practicing humility as pagans. *St. Francis de Sales*

Of St. Vincent de Paul it truly can be said that he possessed real humility. He always did his utmost to remain hidden and unknown, to lower himself in the eyes of others and to be despised. He never let slip by any occasion of humiliation, but always accepted it willingly and joyfully.

All this he did because he really thought very little of himself and in order to imitate the Son of God Who, as he said in a conference one day, "being the splendor and glory of His Father, not content to lead a life of continual humiliation, willed, even after His death to remain before our eyes in a state of ignominy—nailed to the Cross." St. Vincent's humility was, indeed, so sincere that it showed in his eyes, his face and his whole bearing.

MARCH

Mortification

If anyone wishes to come after Me, let him deny himself, and take up his cross, and follow Me.   Matt. 16:24

1. According to what Jesus Christ Himself said, he who wishes to follow Him must deny himself, that is, deny his senses, mortify his passions, his will, his judgment and all his natural desires, for the love of God. These sacrifices are certainly very pleasing to God. We must never tire of offering them up if one should already have one foot in heaven—so to speak—and were to neglect this exercise for the period of time it would take to put his other foot in, he would be in danger of losing his soul!   *St. Vincent de Paul*

St. John Climacus relates that the ancient Fathers, although quite advanced in perfection, practiced self-abnegation. "Even though one is well advanced in virtue," the saint said, "should he stop mortifying himself, he soon would lose his modesty and virtue—just as fertile soil quickly becomes dry and arid and produces nothing but thorns and thistles if it is not cultivated."

✠

2. Our practice of mortification should be the gauge with which to measure our advancement

toward spiritual perfection. We must hold for certain, that the more we mortify ourselves, the more we advance toward perfection. *St. Jerome*

Whenever St. Francis Borgia used to hear someone referred to as a saint, he would reply, "He is one, if he denies himself." In fact, he himself became such a great saint because he denied himself to such an extent that if even a single day passed without his making a mortification, whether spiritual or physical, he considered it lost.

A young monk once asked one of the older ones why there are so many who aspire to sanctity, but so few who reach it. "Ah," the older monk replied, "the reason is simple: to become perfect one must die completely to his own inclinations, and few there are who reach this goal."

✠

3. To conquer ourselves and daily to advance in fortitude and perfection must be our principal concern. Above all, we must apply ourselves to overcome our little temptations to anger, suspicion, jealousy, envy, insincerity, vanity, inordinate attachments, evil thoughts, and so forth. Only thus can we acquire the strength to overcome the bigger temptations. *St. Francis de Sales*

An elderly monk was once asked how he could tolerate the loud cries of some nearby shepherds. "To tell you the truth," he replied, "I felt like saying something, but then I thought to myself: If I cannot stand this little bother now, how will I be able to bear greater troubles when they come my way?"

St. Francis Xavier did likewise and was wont to say that we should not deceive ourselves: "He who cannot deny himself in little things will not be able to do so in big things."

✠

4. He who gives little importance to exterior mortifications, claiming that interior mortifications are more perfect, clearly shows that he is not mortified at all, exteriorly or interiorly.
St. Vincent de Paul

St. Vincent was always severe with himself and treated his body with great severity. Every morning, upon arising, he would scourge himself. He had begun this practice before founding his Congregation and he never desisted— not even when making tiresome trips or recovering from some illness.

All during his life, the saint slept on a straw mattress and rose with the community every morning, despite the fact that he was always the last to retire, and at times, because of his infirmities, was not able to sleep even two hours a night. Hence, very frequently during the day he would be tormented by drowsiness, but he would dispel it by standing or by taking some uncomfortable position. In the winter he would voluntarily suffer great cold and in the summer great heat. Moreover, he sought after and embraced all the sufferings he could, always being careful not to let any occasions of merit slip by him.

✠

5. Mortification of the palate is the ABC's of the spiritual life. He who is unable to overcome gluttony will find it hard to overcome the other vices, which are more difficult to conquer.
St. Vincent de Paul

St. Francis Xavier declared a continuous and perpetual war against the desires of his palate. He never ate his fill of anything, not even of bread. He never ate or drank for pleasure, but only for pure necessity.

✠

6. Without a doubt, one of the things which keeps us from attaining perfection is our tongue. When one has reached the point of no longer committing faults in speech, he has surely reached perfection, as was said by the Holy Spirit. The worst defect in talking is talking too much. Hence, in speech be brief and virtuous, brief and gentle, brief and simple, brief and charitable, brief and amiable. *St. Francis de Sales*

St. Ignatius Loyola succeeded so well in moderating his tongue that his speech was simple, grave, prudent and brief.

St. John Berchmans was a young man of few words; he spoke prudently and was never heard to utter useless words or words contrary to the Rule. There was a good reason for everything he said. When asked as to how he managed never to make a mistake in speaking, he answered: "I never say anything without first thinking it over and asking God's help in order not to say anything which would be displeasing to Him." He was never known to break the silence. When questioned as to how he could observe this rule so perfectly, he answered: "This is what I do: I humbly greet whomever I meet; if someone asks for something, I respond at once; if someone asks me a question, I listen and then answer with as few words as possible, avoiding any superfluous words."

One of the many praises St. Jerome had for his disciple, St. Paula, was that she was as ready to listen as she was slow to speak.

☖

7. It is a common teaching of the Saints that one of the principal means of leading a good and exemplary life is certainly modesty and the mortification of the eyes. Just as there is nothing better than modesty to preserve devotion in a soul and to edify one's neighbor, so too, there is nothing worse than immodesty and licentious glances to expose a person to the danger of becoming lax and loose in morals. *St. Alphonsus Rodriguez*

It is said that St. Bernardine of Siena was so modest that his presence alone was sufficient to make his companions act mannerly. It was enough to say: "Bernardine is coming," and they would all become modest and dignified.

Surio tells us that many Gentiles were converted and became Christians simply upon seeing the modesty of St. Lucian the martyr.

✠

8. Believe me, the mortification of the senses is worth much more than the wearing of a chain and a hair shirt. *St. Francis de Sales*

While St. Catherine of Siena's relatives celebrated Mardi Gras, she refused to do so, saying that since she had no other love but God, so also would she enjoy only that which pleased Him. Jesus then appeared to her and, in the presence of the Blessed Virgin and several saints, wedded her to Himself.

St. Louis Gonzaga mortified his eyes in a marvellous manner. We read that during his life he never looked into the face of a woman. Hence, when word was spread that the empress, whose page he had been for two years, was arriving in Rome, someone told him he would now see her again. "But," he said, "I shall only be able to recognize her voice, since I know not what she looks like."

✠

9. Some persons are so inclined to mortify themselves that at every opportunity they have, they do so. What a beautiful practice this is, and how profitable! *St. Alphonsus Rodriguez*

Mortification

Sister Joan Mary of the Blessed Trinity, a discalced Carmelite Nun, had the beautiful habit of seeking every occasion to mortify herself. In food and drink she sought the most insipid; in the choice of clothes or cell, the poorest; in work, the heaviest. As for her inclinations, she never satisfied them. In other words, she always chose what was most uncomfortable and displeasing to her, seeking in all things only to please, honor and glorify God.

✠

10. One's virtuous exterior behavior depends on how much he has mortified his interior inclinations; and the more he mortifies his interior, the more perfect, amiable, and serene will be his comportment. *St. Teresa of Avila*

Whenever someone would ask St. Philip Neri what one must do to become a saint he would answer while placing his fingers on his forehead, "Give me these four fingers and I'll make you a saint". And to a penitent who frequently asked permission to scourge himself the saint answered, "Why should you beat your shoulders when it is your head that is hard?" The saint was wont to say that sanctity consists entirely of denying one's own will and judgment.

✠

11. Profit is derived not so much from mortification itself as from knowing how to mortify oneself, that is, knowing how to choose the best

mortifications, those most repugnant to our natural inclinations. Some are prone to fast, and even though this may be difficult, they willingly undertake this suffering because they are thus inclined. But then these same persons are so sensitive that if their honor and reputation should be subjected to the least ridicule, or if they should not be given due attention, they immediately lose their peace, begin to complain and make life miserable. Such, instead, are the mortifications they should embrace with great love, if they desire to make real progress in perfection. *St. Francis de Sales*

A religious Priest was once given the duty of assisting the cook. Because he felt such a great repugnance toward this duty and in order to overcome this temptation, he made a vow before a crucifix to remain in that office for the rest of his life, if his superiors would permit him. With these and similar victories he attained such a degree of perfection, that no matter how repugnant to his senses a duty might be, he felt that with the grace of God he would be able to perform it with ease.

☩

12. The mortifications which come to us either from God or from man through God's permission always are more precious than those born of our own will; for, as a rule, the less satisfaction or personal choice involved, the more pleasing the mor-

Mortification

tification to God and the more profitable for our soul. *St. Francis de Sales*

In the lives of the Fathers we read that an elderly monk was told of the high degree of virtue a young monk had reached. The elderly monk, desirous of testing the younger one's virtue, went to visit the latter and, upon entering his orderly and well-cared for garden, began to swing his staff, knocking off the head and leaves of all the plants. Afterwards, according to the custom of the monks, he began to recite the psalms with the younger monk. At the end of the prayers, the younger monk graciously and modestly asked if his guest would care to remain and accept a repast of the few greens still intact in the garden. Astonished, the elderly monk embraced him, crying: "Now indeed, my son, am I convinced that you are dead to all inclinations as I had been told!"

✠

13. The more one mortifies his natural inclinations, the more he renders himself capable of receiving divine inspirations and of progressing in virtue. *St. Francis de Sales*

The celebrated Father Lainez, a companion of St. Ignatius, reached a high degree of purity of mind and an unshakable peace of soul through this practice.

✠

14. Ordinarily, most Christians simply snip at their defects, without uprooting them. They may do something about their spiritual ills, but only a few reach the point of using the scalpel to remove completely from their hearts that which is unsuitable.
St. Francis de Sales

St. Jerome relates that, from her youth, St. Paula was to be admired for practicing this type of mortification. Moreover, as she grew older she increased her mortifications and was ever on the alert to eradicate from her heart whatever might try to take root there that was superfluous or unsuited to her state in life. While her husband lived, she always led such a well-regulated life as to be a model to the matrons of Rome, and no one ever was able to say anything against her. When God called her husband to Himself, freed from worldly obligations, she embraced a very austere life and was faithful to it as long as she lived.

✠

15. He who wishes to progress in perfection must use particular diligence not to let himself be carried away by his passions which, so to speak, with one hand destroy the spiritual edifice being constructed by the other. But in order to be successful, one must start eradicating the roots of these

Mortification

passions while they are still tender, because once they have taken root, there is almost no remedy for them. *St. Vincent de Paul*

St. Dorotheus narrates that one day, while an old monk was traveling through the woods with one of his disciples, he commanded the latter to uproot several cypress trees. First he pointed to one that was but a little shoot; then to one that was beginning to take root; next to one that was already a tree, and finally to one that was a full-grown tree. The disciple then began to uproot them. The first one he picked up with one hand and with no difficulty whatsoever; the second he uprooted with the same hand, but with some difficulty. In order to uproot the third he had to use both hands and pull several times with all his might; but when he tried to uproot the full-grown tree, try as he might, with all his strength and in every conceivable way, he could not move the tree a single bit. Thereupon the saintly old monk said: "This, my son, is precisely what happens with our passions. When they make their first appearance, a little vigilance and some mortifications on the part of the one tempted and he will succeed in overcoming them and eradicating them, but if we let them take root in our soul, no human strength will be able to overcome them—only the omnipotent hand of God. My son, if you wish to acquire virtue, watch the first movements of your soul, and study to repress them instantly."

☖

16. Many take upon themselves indiscreet penances and many other imprudent exercises of their own will, thus placing their entire confidence

in them and believing that these will sanctify them. If only they would use half of that zeal to mortify their inclinations and passions, they would, through this means, gain more profit in a month than in many years with all their other practices.
St. John of the Cross

When St. Mary Magdalene de Pazzi was novice Mistress, she sought, above all else, to accustom her novices to mortify their passions and desires. If she saw one too inclined to prayer, she would send her to do some work. On another, who was inclined to external activities, she would impose prayer or other interior exercises. To those who wanted to do a great many mortifications, she would advise just an *Our Father* and a *Hail Mary*. Among other things, the Saint ordered one of her novices to burn a manuscript of spiritual exercises which she had written and in which she took a certain pride. Thus she helped them to overcome their inclinations as well as their judgment and will.

☩

17. The most important thing upon which to concentrate in order to mortify it and eradicate it entirely is our predominant passion, that is, that affection, desire, inclination, vice or bad habit which drags us down and most frequently causes us to fall into sin. Once this king of our faults has been conquered, the battle will be won. And unless we conquer it, we will not make much progress toward perfection. *St. Alphonsus Rodriguez*

Mortification

St. Ignatius would frequently say to one of his young religious who was by nature impetuous: "My son, overcome this passion, and your crown in heaven will be more resplendent than that of many whose nature is meeker than yours." One day one of the Priests accused this young religious of being impossible to deal with. "Slowly, my son," replied St. Ignatius, "because I feel that he has made more progress in a few months, than so-and-so, who is by nature much meeker than he, has done in a year's time." St. Ignatius himself was, by nature, choleric, but he combatted this predominant fault so energetically that, with God's grace, he overcame it and changed so radically as to be regarded by all as phlegmatic.

St. Francis de Sales confessed that the two predominating passions he had most difficulty in overcoming were love and anger. Love he overcame by diverting his mind and giving himself another object to love, "because," as he said, "since the soul cannot stay without a love, the whole secret of success consists in giving it only what is good, pure, and holy." As to anger, he declared open war on it and never gave in to it. Thus, although he was by nature irascible, he was considered naturally meek.

✠

18. Every time one feels moved by an ardent desire to perform some deed, even though holy and important, he should put it off until he is certain that he has reached a stage of tranquillity and holy indifference in its regard, so that his self-love will not unconsciously taint his pure intention.

St. Vincent de Paul

On one of his trips, St. Francis de Sales went to visit St. Jane Frances de Chantal, who was eagerly awaiting him in order to confer with him about her spiritual needs. It had been three years and a half since they had spoken together because of the great many things occupying his time. Upon seeing her, the holy prelate, asked: "My dear Mother, since we now have a few free hours, which one of us will speak first?" "I will," she immediately answered, "because my soul certainly needs guidance." Whereupon, in order to correct her anxiety to speak to him, which she revealed by her quick answer, he said: "Why, Mother, do you still have desires and preferences? I thought I would find you more supernatural. Let us, then, defer speaking of you until we are in Anecy, and for now discuss the affairs of our Congregation." The good, holy Mother, therefore, without a word, set aside her personal matters and, with perfect tranquillity, discussed the affairs of the Congregation with the Saint for about four hours. Then he left.

☩

19. Never relax, for you will not attain to the possession of true spiritual delights if first you do not learn to deny your every desire.

St. John of the Cross

St. Macarius of Alexandria, we are told by Eriberto Rosveido, being greatly tormented by sleepiness, for a long time slept with his head against the wall to overcome this inclination. The same saint also suffered many temptations of the senses. Because of this, he stayed near a marsh for a long period and exposed his chest and back to the bites of mosquitoes which, in that part of the country, are as large as wasps. As a consequence of the innumerable bites, he looked worse than a leper. Moreover, this saint relates about himself that he never took enough food to satisfy himself fully. Mortifying his senses in this way, he merited many graces from God, and so much did he advance in his knowledge of and union with God, that he would spend entire days and nights in continuous and blissful contemplation.

✠

20. Some subordinate their progress in perfection, which consists in denying their desires and and likings out of love for God, to their own tastes and whims. So strong is this inclination that even if they are commanded by obedience to do something which is to their liking, they immediately lose their desire for it, and all interest in it, because their one desire is to do their own will. The saints did not act this way. *St. John of the Cross*

The Capuchin Brother, Blessed Seraphim, once confided to a friend that he would have liked to remain in the house of Loreto or in Rome in order to serve as many Masses as possible. Upon being told that if he but asked the favor, his Superiors would readily grant him his wish, he answered: "Oh! never! No matter how holy a desire may be, it must never be defiled by one's own will."

Another Capuchin, St. Felix, never did anything without the permission and expressed will of his superior, even though his duty of seeking alms allowed him some freedom.

And his superiors, knowing St. Felix's integrity and virtue, would often leave it up to him to dispose freely of the things received. But the saint, instead of deriving satisfaction from this liberty, saw in it a reason for sadness and grief for he was unable to practice that entire submission and dependence which he so ardently desired, and was obliged to do his own will, which he greatly abhorred.

☪

21. If we do not use great care to mortify our will, there are many things which can deprive us of the holy freedom of spirit that we are seeking in order to fly more freely to our Creator, without always being bogged down with the clay of this earth. Moreover, there can never be solid virtue in a soul that is attached to its own will.

St. Teresa of Avila

One day St. Mary Magdalene de Pazzi said she desired only one thing from God: that He deprive her of her will, because she knew that she was not progressing sufficiently in the acquisition of those virtues which render a soul pleasing to God. After saying this she turned her eyes toward heaven and was rapt into ecstacy. Then God showed her the immense damage done to souls, especially religious, when they do their own will, which they have consecrated to Him by vow. After this vision, St. Mary Magdalene made the resolution always to do God's will and never her own.

Mortification

✠

22. In all things, always strive to mortify and deny your will and never satisfy it, if possible. Accustom yourself, therefore, to desire and enjoy having it frequently opposed. And when someone contradicts you, whether in material or spiritual matters, prefer to follow the will of the other person as long as it is good, even though your own may appear better to you. The harm done to you by contending with another will always be greater than the usefulness which might come from the willful practice of virtue against another's desires.

St. Vincent de Paul

It was thus that St. Catherine of Genoa always acted, happy to submit her will to that of others. In fact, as soon as she realized that she desired something, she would do the exact opposite.

Whenever Father Thomas Sanchez went to make a request of his superior, he would first pray to Our Lord that his request would not be granted if what he was about to ask was inspired by self-love and egotism.

✠

23. You should never let a day pass without denying your will. If you should ever spend a day

without so doing, you may truly say that for that day you did not live as a religious.

St. John Climacus

St. Mary Magdalene de Pazzi always did her utmost to deny her own will, regarding as wasted the day in which, in some way, she did not deny it or go against it.

✠

24. Do you know what is the highest degree of abnegation of the will? It is doing what the others want, without any resistance.

St. Francis de Sales

When visiting one of the monasteries of his diocese, St. Basil asked the Abbot if he had any monk who showed more than the others that he was among the number of the elect. The Abbot presented him with one who was very simple. The saint ordered the monk to bring a basin of water, which he did immediately. Then St. Basil commanded him to be seated and he began to wash the monk's feet. The latter allowed him to do so without the least protest. The following day, while the monk was entering the sacristy, the saint motioned to him to go to the altar because he desired to ordain him a priest. The monk allowed himself to be ordained without any resistance. In view of all this, the saint deemed the latter dead to his own will and judgment, and worthy to be considered one of the elect.

✠

25. The greatest gift one could receive from God in this world is that of knowing, wanting and overcoming one's self by denying one's own will.
St. Francis of Assisi

The Abbot Pastore used to think highly of this exercise and he was wont to say that our will is a wall of iron which separates us from God.

Blessed Colletta used to say that it is more important to deny our own will than to give up all the riches of the world. Hence she sought to put this principle into practice with all her heart.

St. Bernard was also of the same opinion and he used to say that all evils stem from one root: the will.

✠

26. Try not to put too much trust in your own opinion because otherwise without a doubt you will become drunk with it. There is no difference between an intoxicated person and one who can see only his own points of view. The second is no more capable of reasoning than the first.
St. Francis de Sales

Blessed Alexander Sauli, Bishop of Aleria, always sought counsel for the affairs of the diocese, never trusting his own opinion. He considered himself completely unsuited for his office, even though he had been an outstanding professor of theology and the spiritual director of St. Charles and was spoken of as the ideal Bishop.

St. Francis of Paula, although blessed with the gift of prophecy, always asked counsel when in doubt, even in small matters and from those under him.

✠

27. Each one has his own opinions but this is not an obstacle to virtue. Only a passionate clinging to our opinions and a high esteem for them are in extreme opposition to our perfection.
St. Francis de Sales

The same saint had reached such a degree of detachment from his own views that he could write to a friend that he did not mind whether or not others followed his opinions, nor did he expect his ways of thinking to serve as a rule for anyone.

Although St. John Leonardi, founder of the Clerics Regular of the Mother of God, was endowed with great prudence and had brought many important undertakings to a successful conclusion, he always depended on the opinion of his subjects when making all decisions, even on those who were young and inexperienced. In fact, he never did anything of importance without asking their opinion and very often he followed their ideas rather than his own.

Mortification

Even though Father Suarez was both brilliant and learned, he frequently gave his manuscripts to his students for their opinion. Moreover, if any disapproved of some point, he readily changed it.

✠

28-29. The best way to overcome this attachment to our own will is to pay little attention to any opinion when it comes to our mind. When our viewpoint is asked on some matter, we should give it frankly but with indifference as to whether it is accepted or not. It is well to accustom oneself to follow the opinion of others rather than our own, in whatever is permissible.   *St. Francis de Sales*

St. Jane Frances de Chantal, who had a quick mind, whenever asked her opinion about important matters, did not trust in her knowledge acquired during her long experience. Rather, besides praying to God for guidance she would consult spiritual directors and persons well versed in those matters. Then she would say: "This is my opinion, but get also the advice of someone more intelligent and prudent."

✠

30-31. Just as one must will only what God wills in order to be a saint, so also, one must judge things as God judges them, in order to be wise.

> Now, then, who knows whether your opinions always conform to God's? How often have you found yourself mistaken in your judgments and decisions?
> *St. Vincent de Paul*

The same saint always showed himself exemplary in the mortification of his own judgment. He was endowed with so much prudence that he was considered one of the most prudent men of his times. Yet, he always distrusted himself and in all his affairs had recourse not only to God but also to man. He would ask others' opinion and follow theirs rather than his own, when justice and charity permitted it, even though they were men of mediocre talent, or his inferiors. Whenever his advice was sought, after raising his mind to God, he would answer modestly, leaving the decision up to the person himself. His way of speaking was: "It seems that this could be done in this way.... For this reason, it seems that this action should be taken...." When pressed for an explicit opinion, he would say: "It seems to me that it would be well to do thus—; to conduct ourselves in this way." However, he preferred always—in fact, he himself would suggest it—that the opinion of others be asked, and that it be followed rather than his own.

He was convinced that the decisions made with mature counsel and the opinions of others were pleasing to God. He believed that when one has recommended a matter to God and consulted with others about it, he must firmly abide by his decision and believe that God will not hold it against him, since he can excuse himself by saying: "Lord, I recommended the matter to You and asked the advice of others, doing my best to know Your will."

APRIL

Patience

> He who does not take up his cross and follow Me, is not worthy of Me.   Matt. 10:38

1. The Cross is the royal door through which one enters the temple of sanctity. It is impossible to enter it by any other way. Hence, we frequently must immolate our heart to the love of Jesus upon the same altar of the cross on which He sacrificed His life for love of us.

Father Alvarez made this resolution: "I will consider every aridity, worry and struggle that comes during prayer as a martyrdom, and, as such, I will endure it with constancy." He faithfully kept this resolution for sixteen years, after which he received many celestial consolations.

St. Teresa experienced great aridity for eighteen consecutive years, and afterwards, how greatly she was rewarded!

St. Bernard used to say of himself: "All the things that the world loves, such as delights, honors, praise and riches, are for me a cross; and all the things that the world considers a cross, I approach and kiss with great affection."

✠

2. If it seems to you that you have not yet suffered any tribulations, rest assured that you

have not yet begun to be a true servant of God, because the Apostle clearly states that all those who wish to live piously in Christ will suffer persecutions.
St. Augustine

St. Athanasius, St. Basil, St. John Chrysostom, St. Jerome, and St. Cyril were accused of many evil things, and hence they suffered greatly.

St. Romuald, accused by one of his monks of having committed an abominable sin with him, was condemned in a public Chapter as deserving to be hanged and burned. Because of this calumny, he was prohibited to say Mass. Although almost a hundred years old, St. Romuald suffered everything with great peace.

When in Lisbon, St. Francis Xavier found that everything was going well with him, he became afflicted. If this peace had lasted long, he would have believed he was not serving God well.

✠

3. Since the Son of God obtained our salvation through suffering, He willed to teach us that there is nothing more fitting than suffering to give glory to God and to sanctify our souls. Yes, suffering for the love of God is the right road. Let us suffer as much as we can, for we will be that much more fortunate. For he who is not determined to follow this road will never make much progress.
St. Teresa of Avila

St. Mary Magdalene de Pazzi so loved suffering that she would say: "I do not desire to die soon, because in heaven there is no suffering. I desire to live a long time because I yearn to suffer much for the love of my Spouse. One day, during her last illness, she was highly insulted. Not only did she bear it patiently but also showed a special liking for the person who had offended her. When one of the saint's disciples expressed her wonder at this, St. Mary Magdalene confided to her that she was happy not to have died sooner, because otherwise she would not have had that wonderful opportunity to suffer.

✠

4. The road is narrow. He who wishes to travel it more easily must cast off all things and use the cross as his cane. In other words, he must be truly resolved to suffer willingly for the love of God in all things.   *St. John of the Cross*

Taulero tells us that he knew a great servant of God who had many visions and revelations, the gifts of understanding the Sacred Scriptures and of reading hearts. Fearing that these consolations would impede him from receiving those of the next world, he begged God to deprive him of all consolation. His prayer was granted. For five consecutive years he had no spiritual delights whatsoever, nor any visions. Instead he led a life full of afflictions, temptations and aridity of spirit. When God was moved to pity at the sight of so much suffering and sent him some consolation, he turned to Him with these words, "O Lord, I do not desire any consolation in this world. I only want You, my Love, to enter my heart. I receive enough joy when Your holy will is accomplished in me." God was so pleased by this act of detachment, that He called him His beloved son.

✠

5. You repay with some tribulation, O Lord, him who does You a service. What an inestimable reward this is for those who truly love You, if they knew its value! *St. Teresa of Avila*

Whenever the Venerable Monsignor di Palafox had to suffer some insult, calumny or trial after having done a good work, he would take it as a special grace from God and say: "This is a sign that, since I receive no reward upon this earth, God wishes to reward me fully in heaven."

✠

6. O you who want to walk in security and in consolation, if you only knew how pleasing suffering is to God, and how helpful it is in acquiring other benefits, you would never seek consolations in anything, but rather would deem it a great joy to carry the cross in the footsteps of Jesus.
St. John of the Cross

During the "Mardi Gras" season one year, St. Gertrude begged Our Lord to tell her how she could be of some service to Him, in order to make up for the sins committed

Patience

during those three days before Lent. Our Lord answered: "My daughter, you will never do Me a greater service than that of patiently bearing, in memory of My Passion, whatever tribulation befalls you, whether internal or external, and of always trying to do those things which are most contrary to your desires."

One day Our Lord appeared to St. Teresa of Avila and said to her: "The souls most pleasing to My Heavenly Father are those that suffer the greatest afflictions and tribulations." From then on, the saint conceived a great love for suffering and found no consolation except in suffering. And when she did not have anything to suffer, she was unhappy. She admitted that she would not exchange her tribulations for all the treasures of the world. Frequently she would say: "Let me suffer or let me die." After her death she appeared to one of her devotees and declared that she enjoyed as much happiness in heaven as she had suffered trials on earth, and that if she could desire for some reason to return to earth, it would be only to suffer some more.

☩

7. An ounce of crosses is worth more than a thousand pounds of prayer; a day of crucifixion is more valuable than one hundred years of all other holy exercises. It is of more value to stay one moment on the cross than to enjoy all the delights of paradise. *Ven. Sr. M. Victoria Angelini*

When Blessed Angela of Foligno was asked how she could accept and suffer so happily all the trials that befell her, she replied: "Believe me when I say that the value and greatness of suffering is not known. If we understood it well, we would try our utmost to steal from one another the occasions of suffering."

☦

8. A "thanks be to God," a "blessed be God," said in times of adversity have more value than a thousand "thank you's" in times of prosperity.
Father M. D'Avila

While ill and suffering severely, St. Francis was told by one of his religious that he should ask God for some relief. But the saint reprimanded him and, bowing his head, said: "O God, I thank You for this trial which I am undergoing and I beg You, if it pleases You, to increase my pains. What could and should be more pleasing to me than that You afflict me, when this is what I desire above everything else?"

☦

9. If God were to grant you the gift of raising the dead, He would be giving you much less than when He permits you to suffer. In fact, with the gift of miracles He makes you His debtor, but with sufferings He makes Himself your debtor. And if your sufferings should not be rewarded in any other way but to be able to suffer a little for that God

Who loves you, would not this be a sufficiently great recompense in itself? He who loves understands what I mean. *St. John Chrysostom*

This same saint esteemed suffering so highly that he could say: "I do not so much admire St. Paul because he was rapt to the third heaven, as I do for the imprisonment he underwent. Hence, if I were asked: 'Would you prefer to be taken up into heaven with the Angels or remain in prison with St. Paul?' I would choose the latter. And if I were asked who I would rather be, St. Peter in chains or the Angel who released him, I would more willingly be the former."

✠

10. To have everything go along smoothly, according to one's desires and without having anything to suffer for the love of God should be considered a great misfortune not only for individuals, but also for Congregations as a whole. Yes, you may be certain that a person or Congregation that does not suffer and is praised by the whole world is heading for a fall! *St. Vincent de Paul*

That St. Vincent was convinced of this may be seen by what he said when he informed the members of his Congregation of a great loss they had suffered: "After considering that for quite some time our Congregation was going ahead prosperously and everything was turning out well, I began to fear, knowing that God is wont to try His servants. But may His divine goodness be praised for having now deigned to visit us with a considerable loss."

When St. Francis and St. Andrew Avellino passed a day without suffering something for the love of God, they felt that God had forgotten them and had abandoned them.

☩

11. We never have a greater reason to rejoice than when we are oppressed and burdened by sufferings and afflictions, because these render us similar to Christ our Lord, and this resemblance is a true sign of our predestination.

St. Vincent de Paul

Upon seeing the cross on which he was about to be crucified, the Apostle St. Andrew exclaimed: "O cross so greatly desired, sought and loved by me, behold, I come to you full of joy and confidence. Separate me from men and bring me to my Master, so that through you I may receive Him Who, through you, redeemed me."

One day Jesus said to St. Gertrude: "The more you are tried and your way of life is disapproved of, through no fault of your own, the dearer you will be to Me because you will be more like Me. I suffered continuous trials and was opposed in all My undertakings."

When St. Mathilda was suffering during a serious illness, Our Lord appeared to her and told her that when He sees a soul gravely afflicted, He embraces her with His left arm in order to draw her heart closer to His.

✠

12. There is no surer way to know that one is a saint than to see him lead a holy life and yet suffer desolation, trials and tribulations.
St. Louis Gonzaga

St. Ignatius Loyola, being perfect and dear to God, seemed to draw down persecutions upon himself to such a point that when he was away, his companions enjoyed great peace, but upon his return, the community would undergo some trial.

✠

13. If God sends you many sufferings, it is a sign that He has great plans for you and certainly wants to make you a saint. If you desire to become a great saint, ask Him to send you much suffering. To enkindle the fire of divine love, the best wood is that of the cross, which Our Lord used for His great sacrifice of love. *St. Ignatius Loyola*

Joseph suffered many great persecutions from his brothers. This was the way by which God led him to his great honors.

Created for great things, St. Teresa suffered many incredible trials from all types of people, even those who were very good and very spiritual. Many considered her deceived by the devil; others ridiculed her revelations.

Some wanted to exorcise her as one possessed. She was even reported to the Holy Office. Moreover, during the foundation of new convents, she suffered many trials and much opposition from the authorities.

☩

14. There is no better means of distinguishing the chaff from the wheat in the Church of God than the suffering of contradictions, trials and contempt. He who stands firm through these is the grain. He who recoils from them is the chaff. The further he recoils, that is, the more upset and arrogant he becomes, the more worthless he is.

St. Augustine

One day a prominent gentleman presented himself to St. Francis de Sales and asked him to appoint a certain religious to a high office. The saint replied that he had voluntarily tied his own hands in regard to granting such favors, since he had established that all offices should be awarded on the basis of a test of merit. However he would consider his recommendation of the religious, if the latter would present himself with the others. Being of a violent nature and believing that the saint was trying to brush him aside, the man accused him of duplicity and hypocrisy and even threatened him. Upon seeing that kind words did not calm the man, St. Francis asked: "Well, then, do you want me blindly to give him the position? Would this be right?" At that the man became furious and heaped insults on him. St. Francis bore it all in silence. One of the saint's friends, who was present during the conversation, asked him how he could take all those insults without showing any resentment. "Don't be surprised at this," he answered. "It was not he speaking then, but his anger. Aside from this, he is one of my dearest friends. Because of my silence, you will see how much dearer I will be to him." "But didn't you feel anything at all while he was insulting you?" "I forced myself to consider his good qualities which I have enjoyed during our friendship," replied the Saint. Later the man tearfully begged St. Francis' pardon and from then on was a stauncher friend than before.

✠

15. He who is of good spirit tends more toward afflictions, aridity, disappointments and tribulations than toward delightful and consoling communications, because he knows that only in this way we follow Christ and put into practice the denial of self so highly recommended by Our Lord.
St. John of the Cross

Once Christ appeared to St. Catherine of Siena holding two crowns in His hands. One was of gold, the other of thorns. Upon being asked which crown she wanted, Catherine chose the latter. From then on she conceived such a love for afflictions and tribulations that she was wont to say: "Nothing consoles or uplifts me more than trials and afflictions. In fact, if I did not have these consolations once in a while, my life would be the most unbearable in the world. And if God should give me the choice of going to heaven or of remaining on earth to suffer a while longer, I would choose to remain on earth, because I know how greatly glory is increased by suffering."

✠

16. Those who have reached perfection, true contemplatives especially, never ask Our Lord to free them from trials and temptations. On the contrary, they desire and value them as the worldly value wealth and pleasure, knowing that these will make them truly rich.

Tormented by bitter sufferings, St. Catherine of Genoa said: "O Lord, for thirty-six years now, You have been enlightening me and from the beginning until now I have desired nothing but sufferings, both internal and external."

Whenever St. Francis Xavier had some cross to bear, he would pray thus, "O God, do not take it from me, unless You give me a greater one."

✠

17. Frequently and wholeheartedly kiss the crosses God sends you, without stopping to consider what kind they are. For the more ignoble and unwanted they are, the more they deserve to be called crosses. The merit of crosses does not depend on their weight, but on how they are carried. At times it takes more virtue to carry a cross of straw than a heavy one, because the lightest crosses are also the most inglorious, and the least to our liking which always seeks the spectacular.

St. Francis de Sales

St. Francis de Sales undertook many long and hazardous journeys, but he was never heard to complain about the cold, the wind, the sun, or the quality of food served him. He accepted everything from the hands of God, and the greater the insults and ill-treatment he received, the happier he was. Whenever he had a choice to make, he would select the worst for himself.

St. John Climacus relates that there was a young monk who, because of small defects, was given light punishments by his superiors. However, he was treated uncharitably and severely by everyone else. St. John Climacus felt sorry for him and tried to console him, but the young monk said: "Father, please do not worry about me. They treat me in this way not because they lack charity, but because God permits it so that I may exercise patience, which is necessary to try the true servant of God." Two years passed and the young monk was called to a better life. Before dying he said to his confreres: "I thank Jesus Christ and you, Fathers, and I attest that, having been tried by you for my greater good, I was never taken in by the deceits of the devil, and now I die in peace."

✠

18. If we only knew the precious treasure hidden in infirmities, we would receive them with the same joy with which we receive the greatest benefits, and we would bear them without ever complaining or showing signs of weariness.

St. Vincent de Paul

St. Vincent de Paul was subject to long and painful infirmities which often made him incapable of any movement and unable to sleep either by day or by night. Nevertheless, he bore it all in peace, ever remaining as affable and serene as when he was well. One day, a member of his Order was medicating the saint's legs which for forty years were swollen and ulcerated. The religious, moved by compassion, exclaimed: "O Father, how unbearable your pains must be!" But the saint immediately replied: "How can you call unbearable the work of God and His divine dispositions in making a poor sinner suffer? May God forgive you for what you have said. One must not speak in this way as a disciple of Christ. Is it not right that the culprit should suffer and be punished?"

✠

19. There are certain sufferers who become upset and complain more over the trouble they cause those taking care of them and over their inability to do good deeds and pray as they did when they were well than they do over their sufferings. But they greatly deceive themselves, because as regards the inconvenience caused to others, he who is truly patient wants all that God wants, in the manner and with all the inconveniences He wants. With regard to the good works, a day of suffering borne with resignation is worth more than a month of hard work; and as to prayer, which is better—to be on the cross with Christ or standing at the foot of the cross contemplating His sufferings? Furthermore, offering to God one's infirmity, remembering for

Whom one is suffering and conforming one's will to God's—this is certainly a most excellent prayer.
St. Francis de Sales

Although St. Francis suffered severe pains in his eyes, he constantly rendered thanks to God and begged Him to keep him in His holy service. One day Our Lord answered him: "Be happy, Francis, for the treasure of the eternal reward is being preserved for you, and a guarantee of it is the infirmity you are now suffering."

When St. Vincent de Paul was seriously ill, he prayed in a way which was easy and pleasing and at the same time profitable: that is, he would complacently remain in God's presence without forcing his intellect to make considerations, only exciting his will to frequent acts of resignation to God's will, of confidence, of love, of thanksgiving, and the like.

✠

20. Be it known that, in the eyes of God, one gains more merits in a single day through trials given to us by God and neighbor, than in ten years of penances and other practices chosen by us.
St. Teresa of Avila

He does not possess true patience who wants to suffer only when he pleases and from whom he pleases. The truly patient man does not stop to consider the kind and duration of his sufferings, nor who makes him suffer, whether it be a superior, one of his equals, or an inferior; whether it be a holy man or a perverse and unworthy person. His one aim is to suffer for the love of God.

Thomas a Kempis

One day an Angel appeared to Blessed Henry Susone and spoke thus: "Up until now you have fought in the infantry, but now you will go on to the cavalry. I mean, up until now you have mortified yourself as you wished, but from now on you will be mortified by the whip of evil tongues. Until now you have been given milk to drink, but from now on you will be given gall. Until now you have been pleasing to men, but from now on they will turn against you." On the following day, while the servant of God was reflecting on this vision, he felt himself impelled to look out of the window. Glancing down, he saw a goat with a piece of rag dangling from its mouth. It kept dragging and tearing the rag to pieces. Then he heard a voice saying: "This is how you must be lacerated by the mouths of others." And the saint went down into the courtyard to take that rag and keep it as a precious symbol of his cross.

✠

21. God sends us trials and infirmities to give us the means of paying the enormous debts we owe Him. Hence, the wise receive them with joy, thinking more of the good they derive from them than of the sufferings they are undergoing.

St. Vincent de Paul

St. Vincent de Paul clearly explained this thought of his in a sermon. "There was a king," he said, "who kept in prison two men owing him large sums of money. Upon seeing that they were unable to pay their debts, he threw a bag of money to each of them. Both felt the impact of the heavy bag upon their backs. One of them, angered by the blow, burst out impatiently without paying any attention to the bag. The other, paying little heed to the pain, realized the favor he had received, thanked the king, and with that money paid his debt. So it is with us. All of us owe great debts to God for the many benefits received from Him and for the many offenses we have given Him. We have no means of making satisfaction. God, moved to pity on this account, sends us the gold of patience in the bag of tribulations. He who accepts his trials with patience makes satisfaction to God with this precious gold and increases in grace. He who does not, increases his debts and makes himself ever more displeasing to God."

The example of the two thieves who were crucified with Christ also confirms this truth. One of the thieves paid his debt and gained paradise with his patience. The other, with his impatience, added to his debts and merited hell.

✠

22. If ever there should be a monastery without a troublesome and bad-tempered religious, it would be necessary to find one and pay him his weight in gold because of the great profit that results from this trial, when good use is made of it.
St. Bernard

When St. Philip Neri was living at the Church of St. Jerome many penitents came to him. For this reason, the sacristans of that church conceived a great dislike for him and showed it in many ways. Despite all this ill-treatment, St. Philip never complained or gave any sign of displeasure. He prayed for them and always treated them with charity and respect. As often as he could, he would do favors for them. His friends exhorted him to go to live elsewhere, but he refused, because he did not want to run away from the cross God had given him. This went on for several years. Finally, seeing that his charity and humility did not help matters but that rather, instead of changing, those sacristans were becoming worse, the saint turned to God for help. One day he fixed his eyes on the Crucifix and prayed: "O my good Jesus, why do You not listen to me? For such a long time I have been asking You for patience. Why do You not grant it to me?" Then the saint heard a voice within him say: "Are you not asking Me for patience? I will give it to you, but I want you to acquire it by this means." From that day on St. Philip suffered the ill-treatment with greater happiness and to his joy reached the point of not only feeling no resentment but rather of greatly desiring insults and injuries.

☖

23. In this life there is no purgatory, just heaven or hell. For he who patiently bears his tribulations enjoys heaven; he who does not, suffers hell.
St. Philip Neri

When St. Francis de Sales was ill, it was of great edification to all to hear him speak of his illness without exaggeration or complaint. Patiently he bore it without uneasiness. He always took his medicine without a word. Even though he suffered severe pains, he was ever serene and calm, as though he felt no pain.

✠

24. Learn to suffer something for the love of God, without letting everyone know about it.
St. Teresa of Avila

During his frequent illnesses, St. Philip Neri was always cheerful and serene. Never did he give evidence of his suffering, no matter how great it was, nor did he speak of his illness with anyone except his doctors.

For twenty-eight years St. Clare underwent great sufferings, yet in all that time she was never heard to complain about them; in fact, she frequently thanked God for them.

✠

25. He who aspires to perfection must carefully avoid saying: "I was right.... They did that to me without reason." If you wish to bear only "reasonable" crosses, perfection is not for you.
St. Teresa of Avila

St. Vincent de Paul was ordered by a prelate to receive in his monastery a zealous religious and to help him in his plans. The holy man did so and gave him opportune advice. However, a few religious, not pleased with the reformer, criticized St. Vincent to the same prelate. The latter, forgetting that he himself had given those orders, called St. Vincent and, in the presence of those same religious, reprimanded him. The saint received the correction with joy, uttering not a word to justify his action.

☖

26. If we would view tribulations from a Christian viewpoint and if we could rid our soul entirely of all traces of worldly maxims, which impede the rays of faith and do not let them penetrate to the very depths of our soul, how fortunate we would deem ourselves when we are calumniated and considered of little worth. And is it not a great privilege to be persecuted while doing good, since Christ declared them blessed who suffer for justice' sake? *St. Vincent de Paul*

The Apostles rejoiced whenever they were persecuted by the rulers of the Synagogue. And St. Paul tells us that, in such cases, his heart would be filled with joy because with the light of faith he knew how valuable trials and tribulations are.

When told of a grave calumny being circulated about him, Father Alvarez manifested great joy, and said to the one who gave him the news: "Now I see that God loves me, because He is leading me along the path of His beloved ones."

☧

27-28. Moses' rod on the ground was a frightful serpent; in his hand, it was a marvelous wand. Thus are tribulations. Considered in themselves, they are terrible; considered in the will of God, they are honors and pleasures. *St. Francis de Sales*

Frequently St. Mary Magdalene would say: "I do not think there could be suffering so bitter, adversity so difficult or labor so arduous that I could not bear it with happiness simply by convincing myself that it was the will of God." In fact, in the great sufferings she experienced during a trial of five years duration, and during her last illness, whenever someone reminded her that it was the will of God she suffer those pains, she would immediately become serene and cease to grieve.

☧

29-30. When we are made to suffer some pains, troubles or ill-treatment, let us turn our thoughts to the sufferings of our Savior. Immediately our own trials will become light and bearable, for no matter how bitter they may be, they will seem flowers in comparison to Christ's thorns.
St. Francis de Sales

Bedridden, a good woman was suffering intensely. A member of the family handed her a crucifix, telling her to pray to Jesus to free her from so much pain. "But," she answered, "how can I ask to come down from the cross while I hold the crucifix in my hands? God forbid that I do such a thing."

While St. Teresa was undergoing tremendous trials, Jesus appeared to her covered with gaping wounds, and said: "Look, My daughter, and consider the bitterness of My torments. Can yours be compared to Mine?" At this the saint was so moved, that she seemed no longer to feel any pain. After she used to say: "In view of all the sufferings Our Lord underwent, I don't know what I am thinking of when I complain about mine.

St. Ludwina suffered every type of illness continually for thirty-eight years; yet she was ever jovial and happy by keeping before her eyes the sufferings of Jesus.

MAY

Meekness

Blessed are the meek, for they shall possess the earth. Matt. 5:4.

1. Meekness or tenderness of heart is a virtue rarer than chastity and, without a doubt, more excellent than this and all the other virtues, since it is the perfection of charity which, according to St. Bernard, is perfect when it is not only patient but also benign. Therefore we should have great esteem for this virtue and strive to acquire it.

St. Francis de Sales

St. Francis greatly esteemed this virtue. He would speak of it so often and with such delight as to make it evident that it was his favorite virtue. Hence, even though he excelled in all the virtues, he was outstanding in this one. Always serene, his face radiated such goodness that he enchanted everyone. Although he was habitually recollected within himself, when he made it a point to be especially amiable it was a consolation just to meet him and he won the heart and affection of all who saw him. Moreover, his words, gestures, and actions were never lacking in evidence of his meekness and goodness. It seemed that in him meekness itself had taken human form. St. Jane Frances de Chantal said that she never knew a soul so meek, so affable, so benign as St. Francis de Sales. And St. Vincent de Paul attested: "He was the mildest man I ever met. The first time I saw him, I noticed at once in the serenity of his countenance and in his way of conversing a living reflection of Christ's meekness."

The same may be said of St. Vincent de Paul. Of a dynamic, fiery nature, he was subject to outbursts of anger. But when he realized that God was calling him to the religious state, in which he would have to live a life in common with all types of persons, of varied temperament and disposition, he turned to God to beg Him to change his difficult character and make him meek and affable. Then he set himself to work to control the outbursts so natural to him. Thus, through prayer and a constant watch over himself, he succeeded in changing so much as to give the impression that nothing disturbed him, that he was a different man entirely. All who went to him were met with words of kindness, respect and esteem. Always he showed pleasure at seeing them. St. Vincent treated everyone in this manner, whether rich or poor, adapting himself to all.

☩

2. Meekness is a virtue in which nobility of soul is found. Frequently the worldly-minded fail to be meek because they lack this nobility, or possess very little and that imperfect. They might not be the first to use harsh or discourteous words, but if they receive ill-treatment they resent it, defend themselves and give back tit for tat. With this retaliation they manifest an ignoble and low spirit. In contrast, even when provoked by words or actions, the servants of God remain serene and calm, thus revealing perfect nobility of soul capable of overlooking all rudeness.   *St. Thomas Aquinas*

Meekness

The holy Doctor confirmed this statement with facts. No matter to what test he was put he would not show the least sign of resentment. Always and in every situation, he remained calm and undisturbed, no matter what happened.

St. Vincent Ferrer was never known to become angry over any insult or ill-treatment that came his way.

☖

3. Nothing is so edifying as charitable meekness. Like oil in a lamp, it keeps the flame of good example burning. *St. Francis de Sales*

Of St. Francis Xavier we read that his confreres used to go to visit him frequently to enjoy his admirable meekness.

One day, while St. Ignatius was passing a field, a group of farmers began to deride him and call him names. In order not to deprive them of this pastime, the saint stopped and waited serenely until they finished. Then he blessed them and left. They were so astonished by his conduct that from then on they told everyone he was a saint.

☖

4. We must treat everyone with kindness and with those pleasing virtues which spring from a tender heart filled with Christian charity—affability,

love and humility. These virtues are a wonderful means of winning the hearts of men and of leading them to embrace even what is most repugnant to nature. *St. Vincent de Paul*

St. Francis de Sales was so meek in all his dealings that without any insistence on his part, everything was done as he desired. He put his plans into effect and he did it so meekly and at the same time so firmly that no one could resist his persuasive words. In fact, he achieved his aim without anyone even noticing it. He treated everyone with respect and welcomed everyone warmly. For this reason he had such a power and influence over hearts that they would all give in to him. Since he tried to adapt himself to everyone, and make himself all to all, everyone carried out his wishes willingly.

☧

5. At times one word is sufficient to placate an angry person. Similarly one word is enough to dishearten a soul and cause a bitterness which might prove very harmful. *St. Vincent de Paul*

While traveling, three monks lost their way and had to cross through a field of wheat, crushing quite a bit of it. Upon seeing this, the farmer yelled at them angrily, calling them fake monks. The elder of the three exhorted the other two not to answer him. As soon as they were near he said to the farmer: "You are right, my son, for if we were real monks we would not have done so much damage. But now forgive us, for the love of God, because we acknowledge our mistake." Amazed at such meekness, the farmer fell to his knees before the monks and begged their pardon.

✠

6. Since it is impossible for us to go through life without causing annoyance to one another, it is necessary to have a great supply of meekness from which to draw to check sudden bursts of anger and preserve peace of soul. *St. Francis de Sales*

Philip II, King of Spain, had spent many long hours of the night in writing a letter to the Pope. Finally he finished it and gave it to his secretary to fold and seal. The latter, half asleep, sprinkled ink instead of sand upon the letter. Realizing what he had done, he was horrified. Unperturbed, the king said, "Here, let me have another sheet of paper," and he proceeded to rewrite the letter very calmly. Another day, while getting ready to go hunting, he seated himself to have his riding boots put on. After one had been donned, it was discovered that the other was missing. For a long time the king sat waiting while the misplaced boot was being sought, yet he gave no sign of impatience nor did he utter a word. On the day of his coronation one of the soldiers, in the act of holding back the multitudes with a pole, broke three crystal lamps which were above the throne. As a result, oil fell on the costly robes of the king and queen. King Philip, with serene countenance, said: "This is a sign that during my reign there will be the unction of peace and plenty."

✠

7. There are certain individuals who appear to be very meek as long as everything goes their way, but as soon as they encounter some contradiction or adversity, they flare up and begin to smoke like volcanoes. They may be said to be burning coals hidden under ashes. This is not the meekness which Our Lord wants us to practice that we may be more like Him.   *St. Bernard*

Of St. Francis de Sales it is said that the more he was mistreated, the more serene he seemed. It can be said that he found peace in war, roses in thorns and sweetness in the midst of the greatest bitterness. His admirable calm and tranquillity were best seen during the persecutions he suffered because of the Order of the Visitation which he planned and founded, which cost him many prayers, trips and much hard work, and which naturally was very dear to him. This worthy Institute met opposition time and again; many times he saw it on the point of being suppressed. Yet he never lost his unperturbable calm. In fact, he reached the point of praising God that his little Congregation was being calumniated, as this was one of the surest signs of God's approval.

St. Jane Francis de Chantal, on various occasions was mistreated by many, yet she never showed the least sign of resentment. One day, a young man who was greatly upset because his fiancee had entered the convent of the Visitation, went to St. Jane Frances and gave her a piece of his mind. The saint listened with great serenity. After leaving the parlor, she said to her companion who had been present: "I have never heard a tribute as pleasing to me as I heard from that young man." Then, moved by compassion at the thought of his state of soul, she prayed that God would enlighten him. Soon her prayers were answered. Sorry for what he had done, the youth went to ask the saint's pardon and later became a religious himself.

☦

8. When you have to make peace or persuade someone, always be as meek as possible. You will accomplish more and succeed better by making concessions and humbling yourself than by being austere and insistent. Who does not know that one can catch more flies with a spoonful of honey than with a barrel of vinegar? *St. Francis de Sales*

The Venerable Cardinal of Arezzo was outstanding for his ability to keep peace among the members of his household, settling all their differences. In fact, even when he was a simple religious, he was considered extremely skillful at making peace, restoring harmony, and pacifying even the angriest souls. He was able to do this not only because of his great prudence and tact, but also because of his affability and meekness. By placing himself in the position of both parties, he succeeded in moving the most obstinate.

As a child, St. John Berchmans always found a way to bring about a reconciliation between his playmates when they quarrelled, winning them with his pleasant manners and entreaties.

✠

9. If you wish to obtain good results in your work for the conversion of souls, it is wise to pour the balm of amiability over the wine of your zeal so that instead of being too fiery, it may be benign, calm, and compassionate. The spirit of man is such that severity hardens us still more, whereas kindness softens us completely. Then, too, we must remember that Jesus Christ came to bless men of good will, and if we permit Him to guide them, little by little He will obtain results.   *St. Francis de Sales*

St. Philip Neri labored unwearingly for the conversion of souls and he won sinners back to God with such skill that he surprised the penitents themselves. One day a penitent went to him who was so deep in a certain sin that he committed it almost every day. But the only penance St. Philip gave him was to return to him for confession as soon as he fell into that sin, without waiting to fall a second time. The penitent obeyed, and each time the Saint absolved him, exhorting him always to return. With this method, he helped him free himself from that sin in a few months, and not only from that, but from every other, leading him along the road of perfection. To another youth who was leading a very dissolute life, the saint gave the penance of reciting the *Hail Holy Queen* seven times every day and kissing the ground afterwards, saying, "Tomorrow I might be dead." Within a short time the youth changed his ways and fourteen years later died a holy death.

10. He who is charged with the care of souls should deal with them as do God and the angels, that is, by employing suggestions, admonitions, and prayers, as well as great patience and instruction. He must tap on the door of the heart as does the Divine Spouse of souls, and gently try to open it. If successful, he shall joyfully bring it salvation; if not, bear the refusal with patience. That is how God acts. Even though He is the Lord of all hearts, He puts up with much resistance to His teachings and opposition to His inspirations. Moreover, although He is forced to withdraw from those who will not walk in His ways, nevertheless He does not cease to renew His inspirations and invitations.

St. Vincent de Paul treated all those whom he directed with great kindness and patience; especially the scrupulous, bearing with their weakness and listening to them with unchanging patience. Thus he also treated difficult souls whom, he said, should be helped with special kindness, since their infirmity of spirit is deserving of greater compassion than physical infirmities.

In like manner did St. Jane Frances de Chantal govern her community. She wrote thus to a Superior of her Order: "The older I grow, the more I realize how necessary kindness is to gain admission to hearts and keep their confidence in order to see that they fulfill their duties toward

God. And if I have been of some help to those who came to me for guidance, I accomplished everything by means of meek and humble charity."

✠

11. Just as it is impossible to please God without faith, so also is it impossible to be pleasing to men and to govern well without meekness.

St. Bernard

St. Bernard's own experience proves this. When he first became abbot of his monastery, he ruled with great severity and austerity and, although he was held in high esteem by his monks, nevertheless they could not stand him. For this reason Our Lord inspired the saint to be gentler and kinder. St. Bernard obeyed and won affection and exact obedience from all.

Cassidorus narrates that when made king, Theobaldus was wont to say: "With the change of status we changed our resolve. If before we dealt harshly, now we deal mercifully at all times."

Nicetus writes in his annals that a certain emperor, nearing his death, called the princes of the empire and said to them: "As you see, both of my sons are good; however, I consider the younger of the two more capable of ruling the empire. Besides the other virtues he possesses, he is inclined to clemency and meekness, and, if he should fall into some error, he will listen to the advice of others and follow the dictates of reason. The older son, instead, becomes angry very easily and in his fury cannot control himself."

✠

12. I have considered every way of governing and even tried out different methods, but I have found that to be humble, sincere and patient is best.
St. Jane Frances de Chantal

Thus did the same saint act with her religious, obtaining from all of them what she desired. When she asked them to do indifferent things, she was so meek that the Sisters were confounded by her humility. When she asked them to do what was required, she did so with such kindness that one would have had to be heartless not to obey her orders promptly.

St. Vincent de Paul wrote to a superior who had complained about one of his subjects: "The priest of whom you write is an upright man striving after virtue. Before joining us, he was highly esteemed in the world. If now he is a bit upset, concerned with worldly affairs, worried about his relatives and annoying to his fellow religious, it will be well to bear with him kindly. If he did not have these defects, he would have others, and if you did not have anything to suffer, you would not have much opportunity to practice charity, nor would your life closely resemble Our Lord's. He chose rough men for His disciples, men subject to many faults, so that, in exercising patience and affability, He might teach us how superiors should act."

Another time the same saint wrote thus to a missionary who was unhappy over the departure of one of his subjects who had labored with him: "I do not doubt that the separation from this dear companion and faithful friend is painful for you, but remember that Our Lord left His own Mother, and His disciples, whom the Holy Spirit had so perfectly united, separated from one another for the service of their Master."

✠

13. Anyone in authority must never cease to oppose and correct the faults of his subjects and even oppose their opinions when necessary. However, he must always do so gently and calmly, especially when he has to say certain things difficult to accept. Such corrections must first be baked in a burning flame of charity which removes all bitterness from them. Otherwise they will be sour fruits, apt to do more harm than good. Although bitter by nature, when purified by the fire of charity and flavored with kindness, reproval becomes appealing and appreciated. *St. Francis de Sales*

When Father Lambert of the Congregation of the Missions had to correct one of his subjects, he did so with great kindness, never exaggerating faults. Rather, as far as possible, he would overlook them, even if they were committed in his presence.

When St. Vincent de Paul was obliged to correct his religious, he did so with such restraint and such gentle, winning ways, that the hardest hearts melted, unable to resist the power of his kindness. To make his corrections fruitful, he would take the following precautions: First,

Meekness

as a rule he would not correct at the moment the fault was committed. He waited a while to consider in prayer the best way to make the correction, especially if the fault were serious and the person poorly disposed to receive the reproval. When the opportune time came, trustingly and cordially, he would ask the person if he were willing to be admonished, adding that he realized that he himself was more imperfect and blameworthy than anyone. Second, he would manifest his affection for him and praise him for his good qualities, thus opening the way tactfully to show him his fault, convince him of its seriousness and point out its evil consequences. However, he would excuse him, make as little of it as he could and then suggest a remedy. Third, he ended by encouraging the religious, telling him that God had permitted the fault to humble him and give him incentive to strive more fervently to acquire virtue. He was convinced that those who err must be admonished at the opportune time—at the first failing, kindly and gently; the second time, a little severely and seriously, but always affably; the third time, strongly and firmly, pointing out to the person the last remedy, which absolutely must be taken.

✠

14. A superior's only goal should be the love of God and the sanctification of the souls entrusted to his care, which can best be accomplished by being humble, agreeable and exemplary.
St. Vincent de Paul

For this reason, the same saint exhorted superiors to see to it that the yoke of obedience was light to their subjects. He did not want them therefore to assume a harsh, imperious manner, but rather, to be always respectful and loving. Hence, to one whom he had just appointed superior of a house, he offered this advice: "Do not be concerned about showing yourself to be the superior and lording it over your subjects. I do not agree with someone who said a few days ago that to govern well and maintain one's authority, a superior must show that he is the superior. Heavens, no! Jesus Christ did not talk that way. In fact, with words and examples, He taught the contrary, saying that He had not come into the world to be served, but to serve, and also that whoever would be a superior must become the servant of all. Make this principle your own, and then as one of them approach those who have been entrusted to your care. If you put this rule into practice, both inside the monastery and out, you will be happy."

St. Francis Borgia was very strict with himself but very compassionate and benign with his subjects. In fact, although he never forgave himself the least little fault, he forgave every failing in others. Whenever he commanded, he never employed harsh ways but would say kindly: "Would it be hard for you to go to such a place? ... Would you please do this? ... I was thinking of entrusting you with this office.... What do you say?"

St. John, a Prior in the Order of Canons Regular, was one day treated rudely by one of his subjects. The saint uttered not a word. Another religious, who was present at the time, said: "You could have put a stop to such boldness by ordering him to go to his room." "No," answered the saint. "When a house is burning, would it be wise to add fuel to the fire? This good monk is on fire now, and if I were to reprimand him, it would only whip up the flames. When the fire has died down, the remedy can be applied."

Meekness

Speaking of St. Paula, St. Jerome said that she always fulfilled all her obligations as Superior of the Convent she had built and never asked her daughters to do anything she herself had not done first. The only way she manifested her authority was by providing with care for every need of the Sisters and inciting them to the practice of virtue.

✠

15. In religious houses, unity and peace must be preferred to everything else. These two blessings will be obtained if the religious bear with one another, submit to one another and treat one another with meekness, which is a source of peace and a bond of perfection uniting hearts.
St. Vincent de Paul

Whenever St. Vincent de Paul had to correct someone of a defect, he was very careful not to reveal the identity of the person who had told him of the fault. In fact, if he feared giving occasion of suspicion or of aversion toward someone, in order to maintain peace in the community he would rather refrain from making the correction.

As a Novice, St. John Berchmans had the duty of admonishing the others. He declared that he never referred anything to his superior without first kneeling before the Blessed Sacrament and consulting with God, so as not to perturb the others nor be deceived by his own judgment and sentiments.

✠

16. It is very important to make certain that our conversation is pleasing. It will be if with everyone we are humble, patient, respectful, cordial, gracious and yielding in all things permissible. Above all, we must guard against contradicting others when there is no real necessity; and if it is necessary, it should be done with meekness and great tact so as not to upset the other person, thus avoiding quarrels which cause nothing but bitterness and are more the result of attachment to one's own opinions than of a love for the truth. Believe me, there is no greater enemy of good human relations than the one who always contradicts others. Likewise, there is no one more liked by everyone than he who never contradicts anyone.

St. Francis de Sales

Father Lambert Cousteaux, of the Congregation of the Missions, although inclined to severity by nature, showed a great respect and a singular goodness toward all. He was always jovial and courteous in speech with everyone, offending no one. His affable way of conversing won the hearts of all with whom he came in contact—so much so, that they would take leave of him satisfied and content, greatly consoled by his kind ways and by the Christian spirit with which he submitted to their opinions and viewpoints.

It is said that St. John Berchmans never quarreled with anyone. For this reason, all his companions not only loved him, but also permitted him to correct them and guide them as though he had authority over them.

✠

17. Let us strive to be kind, meek and humble with everyone, but especially so with those whom God has destined to be our companions. Let us not be one of those who are angels in public and devils at home. *St. Francis de Sales*

This same saint treated with kindness everyone of his household, even his servants, never being harsh with them in word or deed. He asked rather than commanded and always greeted them courteously. He never complained if they did something wrong when serving him in his room or at table. When he had to reprimand them, he did so with such goodness and consideration that they were abashed and emended their ways without fail. One evening, for example, he had to talk at length with a Marquis about some important affairs and it was dark when they finally finished. In the meantime, the servants, each thinking the other had taken care of it, had left him alone and without a candle. Consequently when the Marquis was ready to leave, the saint had to lead him by the hand through the gallery and down the hall to the door. There they found his servants entertaining themselves with those of the Marquis. While retiring, the saint said to his butler: "My friend, with a two-cent candle we would have done honor to ourselves this evening."

St. Vincent de Paul always treated the members of his Congregation with admirable meekness. He welcomed everyone with a joyful, serene countenance, with warm paternal cordiality, especially when he was sending them to the missions or on a long journey. When they returned he would converse so affably with them and embrace them so affectionately that he moved them deeply.

✠

18. Faithfully check your outbursts of impatience by practicing holy courtesy and meekness with all—whether they deserve it or not—but especially with those who annoy you the most.
St. Francis de Sales

St. Francis de Sales excelled in this virtue. We read in his life that a certain lawyer frequently went to speak to him about unimportant things. Yet St. Francis always listened to him affably. He never showed any sign of being bored or annoyed. Many wondered how a prelate who had so much to do could patiently sit and listen to the man's silly chatter, which was enough to tire even someone with nothing to do.

✠

19. The highest degree of meekness consists in serving, honoring and lovingly entertaining,

Meekness

when the occasion arises, those whom we like the least, those who are against us, who are ungrateful and troublesome. *St. Francis de Sales*

For a long time St. Francis de Sales gave instructions to an elderly non-Catholic woman who was always assailed by new doubts and came to him a few times a day. He listened to her each time with unfailing kindness, never giving any sign of annoyance despite the fact that he saw he was making no headway. The woman did not hesitate to knock at his door three or four times daily drawn by his kind manners. Finally she told him that all her doubts were gone, except concerning the celibacy of the clergy. The saint explained that it was necessary for them to be free from the care of a wife and family in order to serve the people. In fact, he added, if he had had a wife and family to support, it would not have been easy for him to listen to her so frequently. This reply convinced her more than all the theological arguments put together could have done, and she was converted.

Also admirable in meekness was St. John Leonardi. For about forty years he suffered persecutions and trials from all types of persons, yet he never uttered a word betraying resentment, anger or aversion. In fact, he always managed to do something for his persecutors. He prayed constantly for them, excused and defended them, and treated each one as though he were one of his best friends.

☦

20. Do not become upset or impatient at the defects of others, for it would be foolish if, upon

seeing someone fall into a ditch, you should throw yourself into another uselessly.   *St. Bonaventure*

A wild youth was brought to St. Francis de Sales for correction. But instead of being stern with him, the saint was most kind. However, when the young man remained obstinate, St. Francis shed bitter tears and warned him that he would come to a bad end. And so it came to pass, for he was later killed in a duel. When chided for having dealt so gently with the youth, the saint answered: "What could I do? I tried very hard to be angry with him in a way that would not be sinful.... Then, too, to tell the truth, I was afraid of losing in fifteen minutes that bit of meekness which I have acquired after a struggle of twenty-two years. Furthermore, of what use is it to talk to someone who refuses to listen? That foolish boy was incorrigible for he was no longer reasoning rightly. Hence I could not have helped him, and I might have done harm to myself. Charity must be wise and prudent."

✠

21. Upon becoming aware of your imperfections, you should be displeased, but your displeasure should be humble, tranquil and peaceful, never violent and bitter, for such sentiments usually do more harm than good.   *St. Francis de Sales*

St. Vincent de Paul never became downcast or angry with himself because of his defects. He used to say that we should hate the sin and love the contrasting virtue not because we dislike vice and like virtue, but solely for the love of God to Whom sin is displeasing and virtue is pleasing; thus our sorrow for our defects will be peaceful.

Whenever St. Louis Gonzaga committed a defect he did not become disheartened. He would simply recollect himself and say: "The earth has given its fruit."

✠

22. Whoever wants to acquire freedom of spirit so as not to be constantly troubled must not let aridity, disturbances, distractions or upsetting thoughts bother him. *St. Teresa of Avila*

St. Teresa herself practiced this advice. How much opposition and how many struggles, both internal and external she had to face in her life—occasioned by her own religious, by outsiders and even by the devil himself! Yet, in every adversity, she was always steadfast, undisturbed by anything. In this manner she attained to the enjoyment of a great liberty of spirit.

✠

23. Be very gracious and meek, for the whole world expects this good example from you.
St. Francis de Sales

It is said of St. Francis that amid his activity, he always appeared meek, calm and tranquil. He was never known to lose his serenity and good humor, no matter what he was doing.

Amidst his many trying occupations, St. Vincent de Paul never lost his peace of soul. It was amazing to see him receive everyone with the same calm expression, and content everyone, irrespective of class or condition, with great affability and without any sign of annoyance or weariness.

☒

24. Be assured that all disturbing, upsetting thoughts do not come from God, Who is the Prince of Peace. They come either from the devil, or from our self-love, or from the high opinion we entertain of ourselves. These are the three fonts of all our troubles. When such thoughts come to our mind, we should banish them immediately and pay no attention to them. *St. Francis de Sales*

This is the reason why St. Francis himself was never seen disturbed or upset. He paid no attention to the temptations of the devil, was always a sworn enemy of self-love, and was humble of heart.

☒

25. Humble goodness is the virtue of virtues, very highly recommended by Our Lord. Hence we should practice it always and everywhere. Evil must be avoided, but calmly. Good must be done, but al-

Meekness

ways serenely. Follow this rule: that which you see can be done in charity, do; what cannot be done without dispute, do not do. In other words, peace and tranquillity of soul must always take preference over all our actions. *St. Francis de Sales*

Of St. Francis de Sales we read that he enjoyed an unperturbed peace of heart. He himself said one day: "What can possibly disturb our peace? Even if the world should turn itself upside down, I would not become disturbed. Of what value is the world in comparison to peace of heart?" Thus he acted whenever the occasions presented themselves.

☙

26. If possible, never become angry and always reject any pretext for allowing anger to gain admission to your heart, for once it has entered, you will no longer be able to banish it when you desire, or moderate it. If, however, you find that because of your weakness it has gained a foothold in your heart, summon all your will power and see that you set your heart at peace. But you must do so serenely, never violently. *St. Francis de Sales*

This was the practice of many saints, who were never known to become angry. Even in the most provoking situations they preserved their serenity and peace of mind. We think, for instance of St. Anthony, St. Ephrem, St. Thomas

Aquinas, St. Vincent de Paul and particularly of St. Philip Neri. Of the latter it is said that for the good of his spiritual children he sometimes assumed a stern expression but as soon as they were out of sight he would turn to someone present and say, "Don't you think I looked angry?" And at once his usual serene expression would return.

✠

27. The means of overcoming anger are: 1. Forestall such feelings as much as possible, or at least banish them at once by thinking of something else. 2. In imitation of the Apostles when the storm arose on the sea, have recourse to God, Who will restore peace to your heart. 3. While you are boiling, do not talk nor offer any opposition concerning the point in question. 4. Strive to be humble and courteous towards the person with whom you feel angry, especially if he has shown resentment in any way. *St. Francis de Sales*

When St. Vincent de Paul felt inclined to anger, he would refrain from speaking and also from acting, and above all, he would not make any decisions until the feelings of anger were under complete control. He used to say, that actions, though apparently good, when done while in a state of agitation are not fully directed by reason and hence cannot be perfect. Therefore in these instances, in spite of the heat of anger, and pretexts of zeal, we must

Meekness

utter nothing but kind and affable words in order to win our neighbor to God.

✠

28. Develop a meek, submissive spirit quick to give in to everyone, in all that is permissible, for the love of God. To achieve this, each morning set your heart at peace, in humility and charity. Then throughout the day check every once in a while to see if it is entangled in some affection. If it is not completely free and calm, restore it to peace. *St. Francis de Sales*

The same saint's spirit of adaptability was so remarkable that Pope Alexander VII, in his tribute to him, characterized him as having made himself all to all. Among the many proofs of this, we need mention only the following incident. Fearing that he would not live long because of overwork and the little care he took of himself, St. Jane Frances de Chantal begged him to have a little more regard for his health. And he, as humble as he was obliging, answered, "I will do what I can, more because you request it than because of any inclination on my part."

✠

29. A very essential means of acquiring meekness of heart is to form the habit of doing everything

and saying everything, important or unimportant, calmly and without haste. Act in this manner in times of tranquillity and thus you will accustom your heart to gentleness. *St. Francis de Sales*

St. Francis himself practiced this advice in an excellent manner, for he was never known to act hastily. To someone who asked him the reason, he replied, "You ask me how I can remain calm and not become upset when those around me are all bustling about. What can I say to you? I did not come into the world to agitate it. Is it not sufficiently agitated already?"

☩

30. To maintain our soul in a state of peace, it suffices to perform all our actions in God's presence as though He Himself had commanded us to do them. *St. Francis de Sales*

This is the reason why St. John Berchmans always did everything well and on every occasion was invariably unperturbed. Before doing anything, he always prayed to God for guidance and then remained in His presence while performing the action.

One of the Fathers of the desert was asked how he managed to lead a life always so well ordered and serene. He answered, "I often turn to my Guardian Angel who is always at my side. He assists me in my every need and tells me what to do and say in every situation. Hence I have a holy fear and respect for him which keeps me ever on the watch to avoid saying or doing anything to displease him."

✠

31. A great means to preserve continual peace and tranquillity of soul is to receive everything from the hands of God, both great and small, and in whatever way it comes.   *St. Dorotheus*

St. Catherine of Siena once asked our Lord the best way to obtain peace of heart, and He answered: "Believe that everything that happens in this world happens by order or disposition of God, and that He never allows anything to happen to someone which is not for his best."

We read in the life of the Venerable Mother Seraphim that in every anxiety and misfortune, she had to suffer, she did nothing but praise and bless the Lord. Frequently she would say: "God is our Father and whatever He does is for our good; if it were not for our good, He would not have done it."

JUNE

Obedience

All things, therefore, that they command you, observe and do.
Matt. 23:3

1. We all are naturally inclined to command and very loathe to obey. Yet, it is certain that to obey is more advantageous than to command. Hence perfect souls have a great love for obedience and find great satisfaction in it.

St. Francis de Sales

St. Mary Magdalene de Pazzi had such a great love for obedience that no matter what she was asked to do, even if it were difficult, and she herself weary, she never manifested reluctance or gave any sign of displeasure. She accepted everything with joy as though she had been told to do something she liked—so much so, that she feared she was not gaining any merit because of the joy she felt.

✠

2. Without a doubt, obedience is more meritorious than any other penance. And what greater penance can there be than keeping one's will continuously submissive and obedient?

St. Catherine of Bologna

St. Dositheus, not being able to take part in severe penance or the common practices of religious life because of ill health, dedicated himself entirely to the practice of obedience. As a result, it was revealed that in the space of five years only, he had gained a crown in heaven similar to that of St. Anthony.

✠

3. Obedience is a penance of the intellect and therefore a more acceptable sacrifice than all corporal penances. Hence God loves your tiniest act of obedience more than all other homages you might think of offering Him.   *St. John of the Cross*

It is related in the lives of the Fathers of the desert that one day four monks went to the Abbot Pambo and, separately, told him of the virtues they were practicing. One fasted a great deal, the second had given up all earthly possessions, the third had great fervor and the fourth had been under obedience for twenty-two years. After having heard each one separately, the Abbot said: "The virtue of the fourth is greater than yours, because each of you follow your own will, while he has made himself a servant of the will of others."

✠

4. A drop of simple obedience is a million times more valuable than a vase full of the sublimest contemplation.

St. Mary Magdalene de Pazzi

When St. John of the Cross finished his studies and returned to his monastery, it was evident that he had quite a concept of himself on account of his considerable learning. Consequently his director gave him a catechism, telling him to put aside all his other books and read only that. He carried out the directive for a long time and very diligently. Afterwards he declared that with this practice, he had acquired not only a strong spirit of obedience but also many other virtues.

✠

5. To pick up a bit of straw out of obedience, is more meritorious than to preach a sermon, fast, scourge one's self to blood or pray at length, out of one's own will. *St. Alphonsus Rodriguez*

When she was ill, St. Mary Magdalene de Pazzi made it a practice not to accept any special food or costly medicine offered her, but if she were pressed to take it for obedience, she would accept it at once.

6. The best thing for creatures is to fulfill God's will, and this is best done by the practice of obedience, which effects the annihilation of self-will and the freedom of the children of God. This is the reason good souls find so much happiness and satisfaction in obedience. *St. Vincent de Paul*

St. Mary Magdalene de Pazzi had such great love for obedience, which preserved her from the danger of doing her own will, that if at times she was pained at being commanded to do something, nevertheless she would quickly recover her serenity and cheer.

✠

7. He who lacks the virtue of obedience cannot be said to be a religious. And I do not know why one remains in religion who fails to observe the vow of obedience which he is under and is unconcerned about observing it with the greatest possible perfection. *St. Teresa of Avila*

St. Margaret of Hungary, a Dominican, had formed the habit of considering as obliging to her alone and depending entirely upon her, whatever command was given in common to all the Religious.

✠

8. Do you want to know who the true religious are? They are those who, by means of self-denial, have so checked their will that they no longer desire anything else but to follow the counsels and precepts of their superior. *St. Fulgentius*

Blessed Egidius was once given by St. Francis full freedom to choose the monastery and the province he preferred. After enjoying this freedom for only four days he was assailed by a great uneasiness of mind. Whereupon he returned to the saint and begged him to decide upon the place where he was to remain until his death. Otherwise the possession of that freedom would deprive him of his peace of mind.

✠

9. Everyone, upon entering religion, should leave his will outside the door, so as to have no other will than God's. *St. Francis de Sales*

St. Dositheus could say of himself that from the moment he entered religion he gave up his will entirely, submitting it to his superior to whom he revealed his every temptation and desire. He used to say that by this means he had acquired such peace of heart and tranquillity of mind that nothing could ever disturb him.

✠

10. No religious ever became a saint without obeying. *St. Francis de Sales*

One of his lay Brothers being gravely ill, St. Bernard visited him and encouraged him to be cheerful, for soon he would pass from his labors to his eternal repose. "Yes," answered the Brother, "I trust in the Divine Mercy, and I feel certain that soon I will go to enjoy God." Fearing that this was presumption, the Saint reproached him thus: "What are you saying, Brother? You were once so poor that you had nothing to live on, until God brought you

Obedience

here, where you have lived so well, and now, instead of acknowledging this blessing, do you presume to be given His Kingdom as though it were your inheritance?" "Father," answered the Brother, "what you say is true, but have you not taught that the Kingdom of God cannot be bought either with money or nobility, but rather with the virtue of obedience? Well, I have lived by this sentence and I have never failed to obey anyone who commanded me. Why, then, should I not hope in what you have promised me?"

✠

11. Obedience is the compendium of perfection and of the entire spiritual life. It is the easiest, safest, surest, and shortest way to acquire every virtue and reach the goal of our every desire, eternal life.   *Father Alvarez*

St. Teresa was firmly convinced of this truth, and she was wont to say that if all the Angels together were to tell her to do one thing and her superior were to command the opposite, she would always prefer her superior's command. "Obedience to superiors," she would add, "is commanded by God in Sacred Scripture. Consequently it is a matter of faith and there can be no danger of erring. Revelations, on the other hand, are subject to illusion."

✠

12. Since the devil knows that obedience is the quickest road to perfection, he makes it dis-

tasteful and offers many objections to it under the pretext of a higher good. *St. Teresa of Avila*

Because St. Bridget was very fond of doing penances, her spiritual director cut them down somewhat. Although she obeyed, she objected a bit, afraid of losing her spirit of mortification. Then the Blessed Virgin appeared to her and said: "Look, my daughter, if two desire to fast and one of them, being free, does so, while the other, under obedience, does not, the first receives one reward while the other receives two: one for his desire and another for his obedience." Her words enlightened and consoled the Saint.

☩

13. The more clearly it is seen that one is unwilling to submit to obedience in some matter, the more evident it is that the point in question is a temptation. When God sends some inspirations, the first one He sends is to obey. *St. Teresa of Avila*

We read in the life of Blessed Jordan, Superior General of the Dominicans, that one day he had an attack of fever in a city in Piedmont and was taken in by the Bishop. His host had him put in a soft, comfortable bed. The humble servant of God did not want such comfort, but was induced to accept it by a Prior of the Order, skilled in medicine and sent to care for him, to whom he then owed obedience. That night the devil saw his chance and appeared to Blessed Jordan in the form of a radiant angel. Gazing at him wonderingly, he scolded the sick man, saying that he could not understand how he could rest in such luxury, so readily give up his usual penances and think nothing of the scandal he was giving his fellow religious. Then he told him he should lie down on the bare floor, and with these words, disappeared. The holy man immediately obeyed. The next morning when the Prior found him trembling with cold, he told him plainly that he would kill himself that way and compelled him to let himself be put back to bed. But the devil did not give up. The next night he again appeared as an angel and exclaimed: "Oh! I thought one admonition from heaven would be enough to bring you back to your regular observance, but I see that self-love prevails in you. Obey once and for all the voice of God calling you out of this softness, so as to cure you in the austere life proper to your state." Once again the good man let himself be persuaded and lay down on the cold bare floor. The next morning the Prior was shocked to find him again numb from the cold. "What strange spirit of penance is this?" he lamented. But the holy man interrupted him, saying that he was only obeying the warning of an Angel of the Lord who had expressly given him to understand that God desired him to leave that soft bed. "No, Father," replied the Prior, "it cannot be an Angel of God commanding you to disregard obedience. This is an evil spirit who is either trying to kill you or prolong your illness in order to prevent you from giving glory to God with your good works. Hence, the next time he comes, scorn him." With these words the good Prior persuaded him to return to his bed and let himself be cared for. The next night, when the devil returned in the form of an Angel, Blessed Jordan upbraided him soundly. Seeing himself discovered, the devil disappeared in a rage. The saint began to regain his health and afterwards worked such wonders in the performance of his apostolate that it was said his very name was feared in hell and blessed by men.

✠

14. For obedience to be entire, it must be evident in three things: in its performance, in the will and in the judgment. It is evident in the performance when the superior's orders are carried out. It is evident in the will when nothing is willed but what he wills. It is evident in the judgment when his opinion is the one held.

St. Ignatius of Loyola

It is related that the Abbot Silvanus loved a certain monk called Mark with singular affection. One of the monks warned the Abbot that the others felt slighted and offended. Upon hearing this the Abbot conducted the monk to the cells of the other monks and called them out one by one. Everyone took his time to come out except Mark, who hurried out instantly. Upon entering Mark's cell, they found that he had been writing and that, in order to obey the superior promptly, he had left a letter unfinished. With that they all understood why he was loved more than they.

✠

15. Obedience consists not only in doing what we are commanded at the present, but also in the constant disposition to do everything that may be asked of us on any occasion whatsoever.

St. Vincent de Paul

St. Francis Xavier was laboring in India to the great benefit of souls and to his own great satisfaction. But he was so well disposed to obey that he said if, after having begun a fruitful mission he should receive orders from St. Ignatius his superior, to return to Italy, he would interrupt the work at once and sail for Italy.

✠

16. True obedience is seen in the cheerful, unreluctant performance of what is displeasing and personally disadvantageous.
St. Alphonsus Rodriguez

St. John Berchmans was assigned to serve a long Mass at an hour which was inconvenient for his studies, yet he accepted it joyfully, serving it for several months without ever uttering a word of complaint or seeking to be excused from it.

✠

17. The truly obedient person does not stop to distinguish one thing from another, nor does he desire one duty rather than another, because his only concern is to fulfill faithfully that which he is commanded. *St. Bernard*

St. Teresa said that having been ordered by her prioress to abandon a certain foundation she had begun at the command of God, and over which she had labored much, she gave it up at once and felt contented.

✠

18. The perfection of obedience does not consist in doing the will of a superior who is pleasant and kind, who commands in a humble, pleading manner, rather than with authority. It consists in being submissive to one who is domineering, strict, severe, ill-humored and always dissatisfied.
St. Francis de Sales

St. Athanasius wrote that the monks of old used to seek superiors who were brusque, who did not appreciate what they did, but rather reprimanded them, as did St. Pacomius with his disciple Theodosius, in order to purify him.

✠

19. If you do not strive to attain to holy indifference as to who is the superior, do not think to become spiritual and faithfully observant of your vows. *St. John of the Cross*

St. Francis Borgia treated all his superiors with singular veneration, not only while they were in office but even afterwards. When St. Ignatius assigned a lay Brother to take care of his health, St. Francis obeyed him as he would have obeyed St. Ignatius himself.

✠

20. Never look at the qualities and ways of your superior. Otherwise you will change divine obedience into human obedience, that is, you will be moved to obey because of what you behold in him, and not for God, Who is represented by him. Oh, what chaos the devil works in the heart of the religious who stops to consider the ways of his superior! *St. John of the Cross*

St. John Berchmans always saw God in His superiors and never their qualities. Hence he always treated them with great veneration and never felt the least aversion toward any one of them.

✠

21. When a superior gives an order, remember that it is not he speaking but God, and at that moment the superior is but the instrument through which the voice of God passes. This is the true key to obedience and the reason those who are perfect obey so promptly in everything and do not make any distinction between one superior and another. They obey in the same manner both the lowest and the highest superiors, the imperfect and the perfect, because they consider neither the person nor

the qualities of the superior but only God, Who is always the same. *St. Alphonsus Rodriguez*

St. Louis Gonzaga related that he did not remember ever having transgressed the smallest order of his superiors. He was just as submissive and respectful to the school janitor as he would have been to the Superior General.

☩

22. Do you know why many, after being in religion a long time and performing many acts of obedience, never acquire the habit of this virtue? The reason is that they do not obey because it is the will of God, (which is the formal reason for obedience,) but they obey now for one reason, now for another. Thus these acts, not being always the same, can never lead to the habit of this virtue.
St. Alphonsus Rodriguez.

St. Mary Magdalene de Pazzi never looked at the person of the superior commanding her, but saw in her the Person of God. Neither did she ever obey for any reason other than to do the will of God. Whatever her superior commanded her, she regarded as imposed by divine authority. Willingly she obeyed everyone from the Prioress down to the cook. And in obeying she experienced great happiness and delight.

✠

23. If ever feelings, thoughts and judgments against obedience should come to you, even though they may seem good and holy, disregard them and promptly reject them as you would thoughts against chastity and against the faith.   *St. John Climacus*

While preparing for a philosophical discussion, St. John Berchmans was asked to go out as a companion. As he needed the time to study, he felt a little reluctance, but immediately, without giving any sign of it, he overcame it by thinking of something else.

✠

24. Never let yourself stop to examine and judge the orders of your superiors, why they gave a particular command, or whether it would have been better to do it another way. This is not the duty of the subject, but of the superior.

St. Jerome

One summer day during the very hot season, St. John Berchmans went out three or four times, because several religious had asked the Superior for him as a companion. His roommate, feeling sorry for him, told him to be more prudent, or he would become ill. St. John answered pleasantly, "Brother, I must leave prudence to the one in charge; my only duty is to obey."

✠

25. To obey, it is not enough to do what obedience commands. It is necessary to do it without reasoning about it. Be convinced that whatever is commanded is the best thing that can be done, even though it may seem to be or really be the contrary.
St. Philip Neri

Father Alvarez willingly submitted to obedience in all things. He used to say that in his experience he had found that even when it seemed it would be better to do the opposite of what obedience commanded, in obeying things turned out for the best.

✠

26. He who lives under obedience must let himself be guided by Divine Providence through the superior. And he should be as one dead. The sign of being dead is not to see, hear, complain, or show preference for anything, but to let one's self be treated in any way and placed anywhere. See what is lacking in your obedience.
St. Ignatius of Loyola

On the very day that she received the Religious Habit, St. Mary Magdalene de Pazzi humbly knelt at the feet of her superior and gave herself up totally to her will. She asked her to do with her whatever she wished, because she would always be ready to obey her in everything. She also begged her superior to humiliate her without restraint.

In this manner she lived completely docile to her superior's will, promptly obeying her in everything, allowing her to employ her as she desired, without ever contradicting her or showing disapproval of what she said.

✠

27-28. The perfection of a religious lies in exact obedience to his Rule. And the most faithful in observing them will be the most perfect without doubt. *St. Alphonsus Rodriguez*

St. Aloysius Gonzaga was never known to transgress the smallest rule of his Order. He was so observant that he could not bring himself to give to his companions a sheet of paper nor receive a holy picture from them without first obtaining the superior's permission, as prescribed by the rules.

✠

29-30. The predestination of religious depends upon the love they have for their own Rule, and upon their prompt fulfillment of the duties of their state. *St. Francis de Sales*

St. John Berchmans was so attached to the observance of His Rule that during his whole life as a religious he was never seen to transgress it. On his deathbed he asked for the book of the Rules, and holding it tightly in his hands said: "With this I die willingly."

JULY

Simplicity

Be guileless as doves.
Matt. 10:16

1. Simplicity must be held in great esteem by those who profess to follow the teachings of Jesus Christ. Among the wise of this world, this virtue is considered most contemptible. Yet, it is an amiable virtue, because it is the one which leads us directly to the kingdom of God and, at the same time, gains for us the affection of man. One who is considered upright, sincere, an enemy of deceit and fraud, is loved by all, even by those who, from morning to night, do nothing but lie and deceive.

St. Vincent de Paul

St. Francis de Sales dearly loved and highly esteemed simplicity, as he once declared: "I do not know what the poor virtue of prudence did to me but I find it very difficult to love it. It is true that the Gospel recommends both the simplicity of the dove and the prudence of the serpent, but I would give a hundred serpents for one dove."

☩

2. Simplicity is nothing but an act of love, pure and simple, with only one aim: to acquire the love

of God. Our soul is truly simple when we have no other goal than this in mind, in everything we do.
St. Francis de Sales

St. Mary Magdalene de Pazzi once said: "If I believed I could become a Seraph by uttering a word—even an indifferent word—for any other end than the love of God, I certainly would not say it."

☩

3. The function of simplicity is to lead us directly to God without heeding human respect or our own interests. It makes us speak frankly and from the heart; it makes us act with sincerity, without hypocrisy and pretense; and finally, it keeps us far from every sort of double dealing.
St. Vincent de Paul

This same saint always kept God before him in his every action. Nor could he bear to have his religious depart even slightly from this practice. Once when one of them publicly accused himself of having done something for human respect, he corrected him severely, saying that it was better to be tied hand and foot and thrown into the fire, than to do things to please men.

✠

4. God loves simple souls and willingly deals with them. He imparts the understanding of His truths to them because He can do with them as He pleases. Not so does He act with sophisticated, shrewd souls. *St. Francis de Sales*

St. Vincent de Paul was of the same opinion, and he used to say that experience daily confirmed the truth of it, for unfortunately the spirit of religion is not found ordinarily among the wise and prudent of this world, but rather among the poor and simple, who are blessed by God with a lively, practical faith because of which they believe and delight in the words of eternal life. As a result, these good souls ordinarily suffer their illnesses, miseries, and troubles with more patience and resignation than the others.

✠

5. True simplicity resembles the simplicity of children, who think, speak, and act sincerely and openly, without any malice. Children believe what they are told and never worry about themselves, especially when with their parents. Keeping close to them, they do not pay much attention to the satisfactions and delights which come their way. They just accept them in good faith and enjoy them with simplicity, without any curiosity about their cause and effect. *St. Francis de Sales*

Simplicity

In her speech St. Mary Magdalene de Pazzi was as simple as a child. There was never ill will in her words; she spoke always with great sincerity and simplicity of heart, but also with such prudence and seriousness that she was both loved and respected by all.

✠

6. Craftiness is nothing but a mixture of pretense and malicious deception employed to fool those with whom we deal into believing that we have no other feeling or thought than what our words manifest. This is completely contrary to simplicity, which requires our interior to be exactly like our exterior. *St. Francis de Sales*

St. Charles Borromeo was very honest in speech and detested all duplicity. He wanted the members of his household to be likewise, as he once made it clear to one of his officials. In speaking of a certain matter with him, this man let slip the following expression: "I shall tell you sincerely what I think of it." At once, the Saint interrupted him: "So, then, you do not always speak sincerely? You should know that no one can be a friend of mine who is not sincere always, saying only what he thinks."

✠

7. One who possesses the virtue of simplicity seeks only to decide whether it is expedient to do

or say what he has in mind; then he acts at once, without losing time or stopping to think what others will say or do! After he has done what he considered his duty, he forgets about it; and if he should be bothered by the thought of what others will think or say, he banishes it immediately. He has no other thought than to please God, and creatures only insofar as the love of God requires.
St. Francis de Sales

The holy Bishop of Geneva, St. Francis de Sales, once went to visit the Cistercian monastery of Grenoble. The Superior General of that Order, a man of great learning and piety, received him very cordially. After remaining in the Saint's room conversing of holy things for some time, he excused himself saying that he could stay no longer because he had to recite Matins, it being the feast of a Saint of the Order. While he was going towards his cell he met the Procurator who, upon hearing what he had done, told him he thought he had made a mistake to leave the Bishop. "For," he said, "you can always recite Matins as often as you wish, but it is not every day that we can receive such a distinguished Prelate in this desert." "I believe you are right," answered the Superior General, and he returned to the Saint. With great simplicity he related what he had been told on the way and then begged the Saint's pardon for his thoughtless error. St. Francis was amazed at such frankness and simplicity, and declared that he could not have been more astonished if he had seen the Superior work a miracle.

✠

8. Sanctity does not consist in winning the esteem of men but rather in striving only not to offend God. *St. Teresa of Avila*

St. Vincent de Paul once said that from the time he had given himself to the service of God, he had never done anything which could not have been done in public, because he always did everything in the presence of God.

✠

9. When one feels that he has done all God expected of him for the successful outcome of some affair, whatever the result, good or bad, he should keep serene and peaceful anyway, satisfied with the testimony of his conscience.

St. Vincent de Paul

When St. Ignatius had done his utmost to lead a wayward soul back to the right path and was unsuccessful, he did not become disheartened or troubled, or feel as though he had lost time. Rather, happy in the knowledge that he had done his best, he abandoned himself contentedly to the mysterious ways of Divine Providence.

✠

10. If you should happen to do or say something which is not well received by everyone, do not for this reason stop to reflect on and examine your every word and action, for undoubtedly it is self-love which makes us seek to know whether or not what we say or do is approved. Simplicity leaves the outcome of its actions to Providence, to which it completely entrusts itself, without looking to the right or to the left. *St. Francis de Sales*

St. Francis practiced what he preached. He never tried to find out whether what he said or did was pleasing to others or not. And when it was told him that a few disapproved of some of his activities, without becoming upset, he would answer: "We shouldn't be surprised by this. Not even the deeds of Our Lord Jesus Christ were approved by all. In fact, even today there are still many who censure them."

✠

11. Do not stop to ask the why and wherefore of afflictions and contradictions. Just accept them meekly and patiently, satisfied to know that they come from the hand of God. *St. Francis de Sales*

No matter how many trials and adversities St. Vincent de Paul underwent, he never became upset or showed

Simplicity

ill-will to anyone, because without saying much he accepted everything from the hands of God.

✠

12. Constant reflections on one's self and one's actions are of no avail; they are only a waste of time which could be better employed in doing good. Those who keep pondering on trifles are like silkworms that entangle themselves in their own cocoons. *St. Francis de Sales*

To a religious who had given him an account of her spiritual life, St. Francis de Sales wrote: "Your course is excellent, and there is little else to say except that you give too much consideration to your every step for fear of falling. You reflect too much on the demands of your self-love, which, without doubt are frequent, but will never be dangerous if, calmly, without becoming disturbed by their insistence or frightened by their number, you say 'no' to them. Proceed with simplicity. Do not be too anxious to possess undisturbed calm. If you do not have much, why become so upset? God is good. He sees who you are."

✠

13. He who strives to please his God and keep his mind on Him to Whom his heart is drawn, will not have the time or desire to reflect upon himself

to see what he is doing or if he is satisfied. These reflections are not pleasing to God. They serve only to satisfy our miserable love and preocupation with self. Let us face the truth—this self-love of ours is a great intriguer who tries to embrace everything and ends up empty-handed. *St. Francis de Sales*

St. Catherine of Genoa once said that God, pure Love, wants to be alone in a soul. He cannot stand rivals. Hence, when He wants to draw a soul to perfection He counts as His enemies all those things it loves and He sets out to remove them, without compassion for the soul or the body. However, knowing how weak we are, He does not perform the operation all at once, but cuts away a little at a time. In this manner the soul comes to realize God's action ever more and daily grows in love for Him.

✠

14. In order to prevent our self-love from deceiving us when we deliberate about our personal affairs, we should look upon them as though they pertained to someone else and our disinterested opinion were required. Similarly, we should consider the affairs of others as though they were our own. *St. Ignatius of Loyola*

St. Vincent de Paul's ordinary practice was to regard his affairs as though they were another's and the affairs of others as though they were his. When some of his relatives were accused of a serious crime before a high court, they turned to him for help. But for the sake of justice, he refused to interfere. In fact, when some of his friends offered to help, he asked them not to risk impeding the course of justice. In meetings with members of his Congregation, when they had to discuss some business regarding others, he was wont to say: "Let us have as much regard for the interests of others as we have for our own."

✠

15. The displeasure we often feel when the greater part of the day was not spent in seclusion and absorption in God, although we were employed in duties required by obedience or charity, proceeds from a very subtle type of self-love which filters in without letting itself be recognized. It is a desire to please ourselves more than God.
St. Teresa of Avila

St. Vincent de Paul had many heavy responsibilities as the Superior General of his Congregation and an important figure at court. Moreover, he was constantly founding new works of charity and giving of his time to the many who turned to him. So immersed was he in these activities that it seemed he had no time left for himself, and it is hard to understand how he found time to perform his ordinary practices of piety. Yet we do not read that he ever complained of being unable to be secluded and absorbed in God, even though he greatly desired it.

✠

16. What a great good it would be for us if God were to place in our hearts a holy aversion for our own satisfactions, to which by nature we are so strongly inclined, such as wanting everyone to agree with us and wishing to succeed in all our undertakings. Let us pray that He may teach us to find all our pleasure in Him, love all that He loves, and delight only in what delights Him.

St. Vincent de Paul

A young monk once asked an older one why charity was no longer as perfect as it had been in olden times. "Because," answered the older monk, "the early Christians used to aim for Heaven and draw their hearts after them; now everyone bows to the earth and seeks only his own interests."

✠

17. For those who are perfect and walk in simplicity, nothing is small or insignificant, as long as it is pleasing to God. To please God is all they seek and this alone is the reason for all their occupations and actions. *St. Alphonsus Rodriguez*

Hence it is clear why St. Aloysius Gonzaga, St. John Berchmans, St. Mary Magdalene de Pazzi and many others were most observant of the least little rule,

Simplicity

very precise in the fulfillment of every duty and action, no matter how small, and conscientious even in very ordinary actions. It is written of the well-known Father Ribera that during his whole life he was as observant and exact as he had been during his novitiate.

✠

18. In selecting a state in life and trying to discover what he is to do for the good of his soul, one must first divest himself of all his inclinations and generously place himself in God's hands, ready to do whatever He wills. Then, using certain Gospel truths as a gauge, let him consider the pros and cons of his projected choice, weighing well the consequences and judging them in the light of the last end for which God has created us. If still in doubt, let him imagine himself at the point of death or at the universal judgment, which will teach him to do now what he will wish then to have done.

St. Ignatius Loyola

A poor man once asked a pious lady for some clothes and she told her maid to provide for him. However the shirt the maid brought was an old, torn one. "Bring a better one," ordered the lady, "for I would certainly blush with shame on Judgment day if Jesus Christ were to show that old shirt to the whole world!"

✠

19. There is a type of simplicity which makes a person close his eyes to all natural feelings and purely human reasoning, to fix them solely on the holy principles of faith and guide himself by them always and in all things; so that in all his actions, words, thoughts, affairs, and encounters, he never does anything which is not according to those holy rules. This is admirable simplicity.
St. Vincent de Paul

Here, without realizing it, St. Vincent vividly describes his own simplicity, which may be called his special characteristic.

✠

20. Prudence, too, is necessary in life to make us circumspect in acting and capable of adapting to the dispositions of all. *St. Vincent de Paul*

St. Jane Frances de Chantal was outstanding in this virtue, so much so that many bishops used to run their dioceses and many distinguished persons even regulated their own consciences according to her wise counsels. St. Francis de Sales, her spiritual director, and St. Vincent de Paul, who succeeded him as her director, often consulted her about matters of the gravest importance and took her wise advice.

Simplicity 155

✠

21. There are two kinds of prudence: human and Christian. Human prudence, which is also called prudence of the flesh and of the world, has only a temporal good in view and thinks only of attaining it through uncertain human sentiments and means. Christian prudence on the contrary, reasons, speaks and acts in the manner in which Eternal Wisdom, our Lord Jesus Christ, reasoned, spoke and acted. It is guided in all events by the teachings of faith, never according to the fallacious sentiments of the world and the weak light of one's own intellect. *St. Vincent de Paul*

St. Vincent de Paul employed nothing but Christian prudence. For this reason he possessed it in a very solid and rare degree. Although he had a keen mind which plumbed the depths of things and saw clearly their significance, he never trusted his own opinion, until he saw it to be in conformity to the teachings of Our Savior. He never did anything important or gave any advice or answers without first turning to Jesus Christ and finding some saying or act of His upon which accurately to base his decision.

✠

22. Let us be wary of human feelings, because frequently, under the pretext of zeal or the glory

of God, they make us undertake projects which neither come from God nor have His blessing.

St. Vincent de Paul

A member of his Congregation wrote to St. Vincent de Paul to say that it would be well to begin the missions among the well-to-do people. But the Saint answered: "It seems to me that your designs are human and contrary to Christian simplicity. God forbid that we should do anything for such low reasons. Divine Goodness requires of us never to do things to be seen and praised, but rather for God alone."

✠

23. Ah, we love ourselves too much, and we have too much human prudence to relinquish any reasons of ours! What a great mistake this is! The saints did not act thus! *St. Teresa of Avila*

St. Francis Xavier was going to India with the title of Apostolic Delegate. On the ship he washed his own clothes. When someone advised him that this was detrimental to his dignity, he answered that the only thing he considered degrading and unworthy of a Christian was sin.

✠

24. When it is necessary to deal with cunning, shrewd people, the best way to win them to God

Simplicity

is to approach them with great sincerity and simplicity. This is the spirit of Christ our Lord, and he who is destined to glorify Him, must act according to His spirit. *St. Vincent de Paul*

In sending one of his religious to a certain region, this saint said to him: "You are going among people who are said to be shrewd. If this is so, the best way to win them to God is to treat them with great simplicity, since the maxims of the Gospel are exactly the opposite of those of the world. And as you are going in the service of Our Lord, you must act according to His spirit, which is all uprightness and sincerity." For this same reason, when after some time the Congregation founded a house in that province, he made it a point to select for superior one who was noted particularly for sincerity and ingeniousness.

✠

25. May God preserve us from bestowing empty praise and flattery or doing anything else to win someone's esteem or support. These motives are very low and foreign to the spirit of Jesus Christ, to Whose love everything we do must be mainly directed. Let us live by the following motto: do a great deal for the love of God and pay no attention to the esteem of men; work for their salvation without worrying about what they say.

St. Vincent de Paul

The same Saint was very courteous with everyone, but never flattered anyone. He said that there is nothing more contemptible and unworthy of a Christian or more detestable in spiritual persons than adulation. He was careful never to praise people in their presence unless he deemed it necessary to encourage them to continue the good work they had begun, or to hearten the weak. He never did anything to obtain the esteem or support of anyone, nor would he permit his religious to do so. In a letter to one of them, he wrote: "I praise your having won the friendship of those individuals of whom you wrote to me, but I do not praise the purpose for which you told me you did it, that is, so they might support and defend you when necessary! Your motive is very low and far removed from the spirit of Christ, for Whose love we must do all that we do."

✠

26. If one forgets to do something he should have done, let him sincerely admit his error. And if something is asked of him which he does not know or does not have, he should openly confess his ignorance or his poverty, leaving deception to the prudent of the world.   *St. Vincent de Paul*

St. Charles Borromeo never flattered anyone with compliments. When an opinion, advice or favor was asked of him, he would manifest in all simplicity his ideas and intention. He never promised anything when he judged it best not to do so and he would say so openly, giving

Simplicity

the reason prompting him not to do it, in order to satisfy the one who had made the request. In this manner he conducted himself with all types of persons.

✠

27. A particular characteristic of the dove is that she does everything to please her mate. When she is hatching her eggs she leaves it up to him to care for her and provide what she needs. Her one thought is to hatch her little ones so as to please her mate and give him offspring. How delightful a rule of life it is never to do anything except for God, to please Him, and leave entirely to Him the task of caring for us! *St. Francis de Sales*

Thus lived St. Vincent de Paul. He was unceasingly occupied in promoting the glory of God and providing for the needs of his neighbor for the love of Him, without thinking of his own needs or those of his Congregation, which he left entirely in the hands of God.

✠

28. There is a type of simplicity of heart in which the perfection of all perfection consists. It obtains when our soul fixes its gaze solely on God and withdraws into itself in order to concentrate simply and conscientiously on obeying its rule and

taking the means prescribed for it, without desiring to undertake anything else. In this way since it is not doing its own will or anything more than others, our soul receives little satisfaction and cannot nourish a high opinion of itself. But God takes great delight in this simplicity, and by it the soul steals His Heart and unites itself to Him.

St. Francis de Sales

St. Jane Frances de Chantal practiced this type of simplicity excellently and experienced its effects in abundance. Simplicity was the virtue she inculcated the most and which she most desired to see established in the hearts of her spiritual daughters. To one of the Sisters who wrote to ask her for a good way of acquiring perfection she answered: "My daughter, the many means you seek daily to acquire perfection, will only make you lose time and become more and more confused. The best means I can teach you is to concentrate all your efforts and diligence on the faithful observance of the Rules, and on carrying out exactly, moment by moment, every command you are given."

✠

29. Oh, how greatly is to be esteemed the generous resolve to imitate the ordinary, hidden life of our Lord Jesus Christ. This evidently is a thought which comes from God, because it is so far removed from flesh and blood. *St. Vincent de Paul*

Simplicity

One of St. Vincent's most cherished and constant aims was to imitate the hidden life of Christ. In fact, he had chosen a way of life apparently quite insignificant and ordinary. Externally nothing uncommon or singular was evident, but his interior life was admirable and wholly divine. He let everyone know that he was the son of a poor farmer and sought to be considered a simple village Priest, hiding as much as possible his wonderful God-given gifts of nature and grace, which made him worthy of veneration. He was an excellent theologian, yet he called himself a poor ignorant student. He made as much effort to avoid honors and high offices as the ambitious make to obtain them. He absolutely abhorred all ostentation and found satisfaction in humiliations and self-abasement.

✠

30. All those who are destined to teach others should constantly endeavor to divest themselves of self and put on Jesus Christ. For in general, things produce effects in proportion to their nature, and hence, if the person imparting the spirit and way of living to others is animated only by a human spirit, will they not be imbued with the same spirit and learn from him the appearance of virtue rather than the substance? *St. Vincent de Paul*

This Saint's principal effort was precisely to divest himself of the human spirit and replace it with that of Christ, seeking to be like Him not only in his exterior conduct but also in all his interior dispositions, his desires and intentions. He desired and exacted only what Jesus had desired and exacted, that is, that God be known, loved and glorified by everyone, and that His most holy will be fully and perfectly fulfilled.

✠

31. God is a simple Being in Whom there are no parts. Hence, if we want to become as much like Him as possible, we must strive to become by virtue, what He is by nature, that is, we must be simple in spirit and action, natural in speech and behavior, without sham or deception. Our exterior must always be in conformity with our interior and only and always we must have no other intention in mind than to please God.   *St. Vincent de Paul*

Such was the simplicity of this saint. Always he was externally exactly what he was internally. Whoever heard him speak knew immediately what was in his heart, because he always meant what he said. In his numerous and varied occupations, his aim was always the same: to please God alone. Hence it can be said that he possessed this virtue of simplicity to such a degree that the powers of his soul were wholly penetrated by it and all that he said and did came from this source.

AUGUST

Diligence

He has done all things well.
Mark 7:37

1. Whatever our works are—good or evil—we are, for we are the trees and they the fruits. They show what each of us is. *St. Augustine*

St. Aloysius Gonzaga wrote in a little booklet the resolution to make sure that his every action was good and would lead him to God.

St. Bonaventure used to urge himself and others to be constantly occupied in good works by often repeating this saying: "Every hour spent in idleness causes us to lose glory in proportion to the number of good deeds we could have done in that hour."

☨

2. It is not sufficient to do good things; they must be done well, in imitation of Christ Our Lord, of Whom it is written: *He has done all things well.* Hence we must strive to do everything in the spirit of Christ; that is, with the perfection, in the circumstances and for the purposes He had in performing His actions. Otherwise, our good works themselves would draw down on us punishments rather than rewards. *St. Vincent de Paul*

St. John Berchmans performed all his actions, no matter how varied, with such perfection that whoever saw and admired his work, the way he did it, and the circumstances in which he did it, was forced to say that it was excellently done. It was not only because of the perfectly upright purpose he had in doing everything, but also because of the care he had of minute details, which made his actions both complete and perfect in the eyes of God and men, as well as highly meritorious in themselves. To cite an example, he did not like to take part in sports, but rather preferred to discuss spiritual things and carry on intellectual debates. Nevertheless, during vacation, when he was asked to take part in some games, in order to please the others he would play. And when he played he was not fussy as to his partner or whether that particular person knew how to play or not, even if he knew that with such a partner he would surely lose. Furthermore, he always put his whole heart in the game and if he lost, he would take it well; if he won, he would remain silent and not show excessive joy, nor make fun of the losers.

St. Ignatius once asked a lay Brother who was doing his work very negligently, "For whom are you working?" The Brother replied that he was doing it for God. "Come now," returned the Saint, "if you were doing this for men, it wouldn't be so bad, but since you are doing it for as great a Master as God, it is truly blameworthy to do it as you are."

✠

3. Many believe that they never do real penance for their sins unless they perform some form of corporal austerity. We know, however, that he does

much penance for his sins who diligently strives to perform all his actions well in order to please God, for this is of great perfection and merit.
St. Francis de Sales

St. John Berchmans did not perform great penances. He made all his perfection consist in doing his ordinary duties well and with great exactness. As a reminder he had written: "My greatest penance is community life." With this alone, he made himself perfect and dear to God.

☩

4. If a man could see what awaits him in the next world in return for work well done, he would occupy his intellect, memory and will only in performing good deeds, not paying attention to whatever fatigue and hardship he might have to endure.
St. Catherine of Genoa

Amid his sufferings, St. Francis wrote: "So great is the good that awaits me that every pain is a delight to me."

After death, a servant of God appeared to a Religious and said: "So great is the happiness and glory that God has given me in heaven for good done, that if I could acquire only the glory that is merited by a *Hail Mary* well said, I would be happy to return and suffer until the day of Judgment all the hardships the world can offer."

✠

5. Endeavor not to appear special, but to be so. This is achieved by doing community life in all things, carrying out every command with precision, that is, in the place, manner and time prescribed, and performing ordinary duties not in an ordinary way—rather in a sublime and perfect manner. This means to appear exteriorly like all the others, but to be singular interiorly—a great virtue and treasure.
St. Bernard

Of St. Francis de Sales it is written that he was most precise, not only at the altar and in the choir, where he faithfully and exactly observed every minute ceremony, but also in private in saying the Office and doing other things.

✠

6. Do not be one of those who think that perfection consists in undertaking a mutiplicity of duties, but of those who make it consist in doing well the little they do. It is much better to do little but well, than to do much but poorly. Yes, little, but well done—this is the best. If we want to progress and offer a more pleasing homage to Our Lord, we should not double our practices, but rather perfect those we are doing.
St. Francis de Sales

A pious religious recited daily the fifteen mysteries of the Rosary, but with little devotion. One day the Blessed Virgin appeared to her and ordered her to say only a third part of the Rosary, adding that she was more pleased with a few prayers well said, than with many said without devotion and with negligence.

☩

7. God does not measure our perfection by the number and greatness of the things we do for Him, but by the way in which we do them. This way is none other than the love of God with which and for which we do them. And our actions are more perfect the more perfect and pure the love of God is with which they are done, and the less satisfaction and praise we expect for them both here and hereafter. *St. John of the Cross*

St. Francis Borgia used to say that although his sermons were often displeasing both to himself and others, because of some defect in the subject or in the presentation, they always brought good results because on his part he did his best and always solely for God.

☩

8. Doing things well consists in doing them with a very pure intention, with a great desire to please God alone. This may be called the form or

soul of our actions. It is what gives them value and, at the same time, makes them easy and pleasant.

St. Francis de Sales

St. Mary Magdalene de Pazzi continuously urged her Novices to offer to God all their actions, even the smallest. In order to fix this point well in their minds, she would sometimes take them by surprise and ask them, "Why are you doing that?" Upon their answering that they were doing it without any supernatural intention, she would say: "Don't you see that in this manner you are losing all the merit? God is not pleased with such actions."

✠

9. On what deeds do all our progress and perfection depend? On all those which fall to our lot to do, but especially the ordinary ones we perform daily. These are frequent, hence in them, more than in others, we must use greater diligence. If we perform them perfectly, we will be perfect; if we perform them imperfectly, we will be imperfect. Thus, the difference between a perfect and an imperfect religious is not that the former performs more and varied duties, but that he does the ordinary duties to perfection. *St. Alphonsus Rodriguez*

Of St. Stanislaus Kostka we read that, although he did only what the others did, he did it so well it seemed he did more than the others.

Diligence

✠

10. Among our ordinary duties, those with which we should be most concerned are the spiritual ones. We should strive to perform them as well as possible and give them first place if necessity or obedience does not require otherwise, because these concern God more directly and more efficaciously lead us to perfection. By doing otherwise, we would draw down upon ourselves the malediction hurled by the Holy Spirit at those who do God's works negligently. *St. Vincent de Paul*

When the prophet Eliseus sent Giezi with his staff to bring back to life the son of the Sunamitess, he gave him orders not to greet anyone he might meet on the way, in order to teach us that when we are occupied in any spiritual exercise, we must not let ourselves be distracted by anything else under the pretext of courtesy.

✠

11. The Mass is without doubt the most excellent and most holy ceremony, the most acceptable to God, and most beneficial to us. While Mass is being celebrated, the Angels assist with attention and reverence, in deep silence and with great wonder and veneration. What purity, attention, devotion and reverence the priest who celebrates it must

have! He must approach the holy altar as Jesus Christ, assist at it as an angel, perform his ministry there as a saint, offer the prayers of the people as a pontiff, intercede for peace between God and the world as a mediator, and pray for himself as any other man.
St. Lawrence Justinian

St. Vincent de Paul pronounced the words of the Mass in an average, calm tone of voice, in a natural yet devout manner, reciting the prayers neither too quickly nor too slowly but suited to the sanctity of the action. His Mass, therefore, usually lasted no more than a half hour. However, the interior dispositions that accompanied his words and actions were unusually tender.

12. Saying the Divine Office is one of the most excellent actions in which we can be engaged, for we thus celebrate the divine praises, a duty proper to the angels. Hence it should not be recited out of habit, but with our complete attention and devotion.
St. Mary Magdalene de Pazzi

When the same saint heard the bell for the recitation of the Office, she would rejoice in the thought that she was being called to praise God. Immediately she would interrupt whatever she was doing. She recited the Office with such devotion, that from her face one could discern the attentiveness of her mind.

Father Suarez said of himself that as soon as he took the Breviary in his hands, all other thoughts vanished from his mind. Hence, during the recitation of the Office nothing, no matter how important, distracted him.

☩

13. The examination of conscience, which all persons of good will make daily before retiring, to see how they have conducted themselves and to discover whether or not they have made any progress, is very helpful not only to control one's evil inclinations and uproot bad habits, but also to acquire virtues and perform ordinary duties well. It must be noted, however, that the most important part of the examen does not consist in finding the failings one has committed during the day, but in exciting sorrow and firmly resolving not to commit them again.
Father D'Avila

We read in monastic history that a holy monk used to say: "I don't think the devil has ever succeeded in making me fall into the same fault twice." The reason for this was that, in examining his first fall, he would be so ashamed of his infidelity, and would so detest the fault committed, and make so strong a resolution not to fall again that no other temptation had the power to make him commit the same fault. All the Saints and masters of the spiritual life have considered the examination of conscience to be of great value. They themselves have practiced it and deemed it the most efficacious means to eradicate any vice or defect, and to make progress in perfection.

✠

14. How can the sun and the moon praise God as the Prophet exhorts them to do? By perfectly carrying out the role God has given them. Thus they render Him great praise. Behold, therefore, a wonderful means by which you can praise God all day; do your duty and whatever else you are given to do well.
St. Jerome

St. John Berchmans was most diligent in performing all his duties. Having been entrusted with the care of his spiritual director's room, he kept it so clean and so well provided with every little necessity that the good Father was surprised. Nor did he ever find anyone else to equal him. Moreover, the Saint never disturbed him or spoke unnecessarily. He also was given the duty of caring for the lamps and not a day went by without examining them and trimming the wicks. In vacation time, when he had to go to the vineyard, he would either adjust the lamps before going or return early in the evening to do it on time.

✠

15. Never think it time wasted that is spent in performing one's duty well. This is something so

acceptable to God that, within a short time, He gives all the graces He would have dispensed over a period of time and often even doubles His gifts of what has been sacrificed for His service.
St. Teresa of Avila

The same Saint tells us that she knew various persons who were for a long time totally occupied in exercises of obedience and charity, yet made such spiritual progress that she was amazed. Then she tells of having spoken with one who told her that for fifteen years obedience had kept her so unceasingly occupied that she could not recall having had a free day for herself. Our Lord rewarded her very well, for in the end, without knowing how, she enjoyed great freedom of spirit and with it all the happiness possible in this life.

✠

16. Do not fear that the duties imposed upon us by obedience, though numerous and heavy, will distract us from our union with God. In fact, when they are performed for His glory, they have the power to unite us closely to Him. How could the very things that join our will to His draw us away from Him? *St. Francis de Sales*

A Franciscan lay Brother, who was a cook, would retire to pray as soon as he had performed his kitchen duty to perfection, and he was favored with many heavenly consolations in prayer. In order to enjoy more he asked and received permission from his superior to be relieved of his duty so as to dedicate all his time to prayer. However the result was that he found only aridity and distractions when he prayed. Realizing his mistake, he returned to his former duty, and once again experienced the lost consolations.

✠

17. Even the smallest actions are important, when done well. Indeed, a small action performed with the desire to please God is more pleasing to Him and gives Him greater glory than an important work done with less fervor. If we wish to advance in union with God, we must try particularly hard to perform well the easy little duties which come our way at all hours of the day.   *St. Francis de Sales*

Of St. Francis Xavier it is said that he always was most careful to do the little things well. He used to say: "We must not deceive ourselves. He who does not become perfect in small things will never be so in the great things."

✠

18. Much more is obtained by a single word of the "Our Father" said from the heart every so often, than by saying the whole "Our Father" many times but hastily and distractedly.   *St. Teresa of Avila*

Diligence

Our Lord once revealed to St. Bridget that He is more pleased when one reads these few words: "Jesus, have mercy on me" with perfect faith and will, than if he were to read a thousand verses of the psalms distractedly.

✠

19. He who has not experienced it will not believe how important it is for one's spiritual progress to be on the alert to avoid committing little defects, because it is by means of these that the devil bores holes through which larger matters may gain entrance. *St. Teresa of Avila*

When superior, St. Louis Beltrando would correct and severely punish the small faults, such as, breaking the silence, and over-sleeping, for he held that upon these things depended progress and religious discipline.

✠

20. Take care that during your occupations you do not forget God, because if He were to abandon you, you would not be able to take a single step without falling. Rather, imitate little children walking with their father. They keep one hand in his and with the other pick the strawberries and currants along the way. Attend to your work, but every once in a while lift up your mind to your heavenly Father

to see whether your work is pleasing to Him and to ask His help. Thus you will perform even the most difficult tasks better and more easily.

St. Francis de Sales

Of St. Rose of Lima we read that in the midst of every activity she kept her mind lifted to God. Hence while reading, weaving, embroidering, conversing or taking care of the needs of the family, always and everywhere, she lovingly contemplated the beautiful face of her Beloved.

☦

21. The main reason we perform our duties imperfectly is that while we do one thing we think of another we still have to do or one we have done already. Thus our duties impede one another and none of them is done well. The way to fulfill every task well is to concentrate solely on the one at hand, striving to do it as perfectly as possible, without thinking of anything else. Once that duty is done, forget it and think only of what remains to be done.

Father D'Avila

At a time when God was giving to Venerable Sister Mary Crucified an abundance of His celestial blessings by calling her to enjoy Him in solitary contemplation, her superior gave her many duties to perform. Yet, she performed them all with precision and great satisfaction, finding time in addition for contemplation. This is how she did it:

Diligence 177

When she was working in the sacristy, she used to say to herself: "Now you are nothing but the sacristan"; and when she finished: "Now you are no longer sacristan." She fulfilled all her other duties in the same manner.

✠

22. Faithfully do what God expects of you each moment, and leave the rest up to Him. I assure you that living in this manner will bring you great peace.
St. Jane Frances de Chantal

St. Jane Frances herself lived this advice. So did St. Francis de Sales. Of him it is said that when he was engaged in some activity or handling some matter, he would apply himself to it wholeheartedly as though he had no other occupation.

✠

23. The second impediment is haste. Avoid it, for it is an arch enemy of true devotion. Nothing done in haste has ever been done well. By all means, let us proceed at a moderate pace, as long as we go forward, and thus we will cover much ground.
St. Francis de Sales

St. Francis himself acted in this manner and so did St. Philip Neri. The latter wanted his penitents to do likewise. To them he frequently used to say: "We must not expect to do everything in a day or become a saint in a month. This is not moderation."

✠

24. The works of God are generally done little by little. They have their beginnings and progressive advances. One must not expect to do everything at once and in a hurry, nor consider everything lost that is not done immediately. It is necessary to proceed slowly, pray a great deal and use the means suggested by the Spirit of God, never the erroneous principles of the world. *St. Vincent de Paul*

The same Saint attended to all his affairs with great composure, both in undertaking them as well as in carrying them out. In fact, he was held to be too slow. However, experience proved that his lack of haste did no harm. On the contrary, to the surprise of many, he achieved a great many successes and in very difficult matters—results impossible to achieve by several people working together. Moreover, in this way he succeeded in performing all his spiritual exercises with devotion.

✠

25. The third impediment is over-anxiety. Diligently and accurately handle all the affairs of which you are in charge, but if possible do not be unduly worried about them. Do not let them upset and disturb you. In taking care of them, never torment

Diligence

yourself, for such anxieties make clear-thinking difficult and prevent your doing other things well. If you practice this advice, you will succeed in discharging your duties very meritoriously for, beyond doubt, time employed calmly is spent most efficaciously. *St. Francis de Sales*

St. Jane Frances de Chantal faithfully followed this advice: "Do everything attentively, but without anxiety and without losing peace of heart." Hence all her undertakings turned out well, and she made the reason for this success plain to her Sisters. One day she said to one of them: "You must know, my dear daughter, that I love our poor Congregation perfectly, but without anxiety." To another Sister who asked her how she could get rid of the continual worries she encountered in her office, she wrote: "If you wish to succeed better in your office and find it less burdensome, you must get rid of your anxiety and solicitude in carrying it out, and seek to act with fidelity together with sweetness and calmness of spirit."

✠

26. To do all things serenely and lovingly is characteristic of the spirit of God, and the surest way to succeed in one's undertakings is to imitate Him. *St. Vincent de Paul*

In this manner St. Vincent carried out every action, whether important or not, spiritual or temporal. His great calm and serenity were even apparent externally.

✠

27. The fourth impediment is a desire to do too much. In the exercise of virtue one should not become entangled in trifles. Virtue should be practiced straightforwardly, naturally, openly and simply, the way it used to be. The freedom of the children of God consists precisely in fulfilling their obligations joyfully, faithfully and willingly.
St. Francis de Sales

Although very exact in her observance of the Rules and in fulfilling her duties, St. Jane Frances de Chantal made sure for her part and advised others likewise not to let such exactness bring on the distress or anxiety which self-love usually causes. Rather she went ahead tranquilly and simply always.

✠

28. One of the many ways of doing everything well is to perform each action as though it were the last act of your life. Ask yourself before every act, "If you knew that you were going to die immediately after this action, would you do it? Would you do it in this manner?"
St. Vincent de Paul

A certain Priest used to go to confession every morning before celebrating Mass. Having fallen ill, he was advised to go to confession to prepare himself for death. "May the Lord be praised!" he exclaimed. "For thirty years I have been going to confession as though I were going to die right afterwards. Hence now all I have to do is to confess myself as though I were to say Mass."

✠

29. Another good method is to give thought to no time but the present. One of the tricks the devil uses to cause souls to lose heart and become lax in the service of God is to make it seem unbearably difficult to have to live in such a circumspect, punctual and exacting fashion for many years. Now, when one takes only the present day account, he closes the door to this temptation and also gives considerable encouragement to our weak human nature.
St. Alphonsus Rodriguez

It is narrated in the lives of the Fathers that a certain monk was greatly tempted by hunger to break the community schedule. Beginning early in the morning he would feel such hunger and such weakness that it was intolerable. But in order not to break the holy custom of the monks to eat nothing before three in the afternoon, he would proceed thus: In the morning he would say to himself: "No matter how hungry you are is it such a great thing to wait until nine o'clock?" At nine he would say: "Just as I've waited until nine I can wait until twelve." At twelve o'clock he would say: "While the bread is soaking I can wait until three o'clock. For another two or three hours I don't want to break the good custom of the monks." At three o'clock, having said his prayers, he would eat. Thus he led himself on for many days until he no longer felt the hunger and weakness as before.

Another monk was gravely tempted for a long period of time to leave the monastery. Every night he would say to himself, "Tomorrow I will leave." And in the morning: "Oh well, for the love of God I will remain one more day." And he did this for nine consecutive years until finally the temptation left him.

☩

30. A serious error made by some good and pious souls is the belief that they cannot preserve interior peace in the midst of duties and difficulties. Despite the fact that there is no greater movement than the rocking of a ship on the high seas those on board continue to sleep and rest, and the compass needle always remains in its place pointing north. Here is the point: we must make certain to keep the compass needle of our will, always in place, so that it will point only toward the pole of the Divine Pleasure.   *St. Francis de Sales*

St. Vincent de Paul excelled in this regard. He never became upset over the multitude of affairs to which he had to attend and the difficulties he encountered. He faced them with indefatigable strength of spirit and worked methodically, patiently and tranquilly, keeping his gaze fixed on the divine will. This was clearly seen at the time he was advisor to the king, in charge of his own Congregation,

Diligence

governing other communities besides, directing organizations and meetings, and handling numerous other matters. Anyone would have imagined him continually distraught, dividing his time between a million different thoughts and cares, and consequently always disturbed and agitated. Yet this was not so. In the midst of this constant coming and going of persons and affairs, his recollection, mastery of self and great serenity of spirit were always evident.

✠

31. Everything we do derives its value from our conformity to the will of God. Hence even eating, if done because such is the will of God, is more meritorious than death would be without that intention. Fix this principle firmly in your mind, and in your every action keep it before your eyes. Thus you will do your work with perfection.
St. Francis de Sales

A certain lay Brother understood this truth well. When he sat down to eat, he would say that he was preaching the sermons of St. Francis Xavier in India.

SEPTEMBER

Prayer

Always pray and not lose heart.   Luke 18:1

1. Nothing is more useful than prayer. Therefore, we must nourish both a great love and a great esteem for it, and make every effort to pray well.

St. Vincent de Paul

All the Saints evidenced great love for prayer. St. Margaret, Queen of Scotland, and St. Stephen, King of Hungary, spent almost the entire night in prayer; St. Frances of Rome gave all her free time to it; St. Rose of Lima prayed twelve hours a day. St. Aloysius Gonzaga began at a very early age to pray one, two or three hours a day. While he was a page at court, he would hide in the woodpile to pray so as not to be disturbed by his companions.

From the age of eleven, St. John Berchmans used to spend in prayer all the time he had free from studies. Any corner of the house would serve for this purpose and at times his family would find him still absorbed in prayer after midnight.

✠

2. The Angels have a great esteem for fervent prayer, and consequently do much to promote it. The devils, on the contrary, have an intense dislike for it and as a result strongly combat and disturb it.

St. John Chrysostom

The same Saint tells us that the Angels greatly respect those who are united to God by means of prayer. While the latter are praying, they stay near them in profound silence, and when they have finished, they praise them.

✠

3. Souls who do not have the habit of prayer are like paralyzed bodies with hands and feet they cannot use. It seems to me that to stop praying is to take a wrong turn, because prayer is the door through which all God's graces come to us. If this door is closed, I do not know what might happen.
St. Teresa of Avila

Her own experience is proof of this. Having neglected prayer for some time, she began to fall into defects and sins which, though small, were not easy to eradicate. In fact, they increased all the time. She herself said that if she had not returned to prayer, she would have lost her soul, as indeed our Lord revealed to her.

✠

4. Despite sins, temptations and falls, the soul who perseveres in prayer may rest assured that sooner or later God will deliver her from danger and lead her to the port of salvation.
St. Teresa of Avila

St. Mary of Egypt confessed to Abbot Zosimus that for seventeen years after her conversion she was incessantly assailed by frightful temptations. Yet, because she dedicated herself to prayer, she never yielded. The same is true of St. Augustine, St. Margaret of Cortona and many others.

☩

5. A man of prayer is capable of everything. Hence it is very important that missioners dedicate themselves to this practice with great affection, because without it they will accomplish little or nothing, whereas through it, more than by letters or persuasive speech, they will be capable of touching hearts and winning souls to their Creator.

St. Vincent de Paul

St. Francis Borgia was a man of much prayer. Frequently he would spend six consecutive hours in prayer, almost rapt in ecstasy. Afterwards, just his appearance in the pulpit was enough to influence the people.

St. Thomas, St. Bonaventure and St. Albert the Great declared that they attained their knowledge more from prayer than from studies. Of St. Thomas in particular, we read that once when he could not understand a difficult passage of the Scriptures he had recourse to prayer and in the height of fervor he was granted a vision of the Apostles Peter and Paul, who smoothed away the difficulty.

✠

6. When one has to treat with others concerning matters of the Spirit, it is best first to treat of them with God in prayer, emptying one's self of one's own mind in order to fill one's self with the Holy Spirit, Who alone enlightens the mind and inflames the will. Superiors, more than anyone else, should do this. They should seek to be in continual communication with God, and have recourse to Him not only in doubtful and troublesome cases, but in every situation, in order to learn directly from Him what they must teach others.

St. Vincent de Paul

When St. Vincent had to decide on a matter, take action, or give some advice, before making a move, he would raise his mind to God to implore His help and enlightenment. Ordinarily on such occasions he would lift his gaze heavenward, then lowering it, would keep his eyes closed a minute as though to consult God within him before answering. If it were a matter of importance, he would request more time, in order to recommend it to God. And since he depended wholly on divine Wisdom and not on himself, he received from God special insights and graces by reason of which he often uncovered things that no human intellect alone could have divined.

✠

7. Mental prayer consists in keeping our mind on what we are saying, and meaning it, in thinking of Whom it is we are addressing and who we are who dare to converse with so great a Lord. These and similar reflections constitute mental prayer.

St. Teresa of Avila

While reflecting on the eternal, infinite God to whom he was praying and on what he considered his own great unworthiness, the Venerable Bishop de Palafox would exclaim: "Lord, do I dare speak to You? You are God Almighty, Creator of the universe, whereas I am nothing, less than nothing, and what afflicts me the most is that I am wicked!" At other times he would say: "Lord, is it not just to love You? Hence how can I not love You? Lord, You came to seek sinners and I am the greatest of sinners. If You abased Yourself so that we could adore You, speak to You and pray to You, why then should I not adore You, speak to You and pray to You?"

✠

8. If, while praying, one reflects on the fact that he is speaking with God, his prayer is both vocal and mental prayer, and can be very profitable to him. But if he neither thinks of the One to whom he is speaking nor of what he is saying, regardless of how much he moves his lips, he is certainly praying very little. *St. Teresa of Avila*

A certain Bishop once saw an Angel descend from heaven and go to gather the tears of a woman who was praying in a corner of the church. Full of wonder the Bishop asked her as she left what she had been doing in that hour, and she replied, "I was saying the *Our Father,* the *Hail Mary* and the *Creed.*"

✠

9. In prayer, when our affections have already been aroused, we should not continue meditating and reflecting, but should pause to enjoy them and from time to time whisper words of sorrow, of love, of trustful abandonment, and the like, to Our Lord, according to how we feel inclined. This is the best part of prayer.   *St. Jane Frances de Chantal*

St. Cyril of Alexandria illustrated this fact very well with a comparison. "Meditation," said the Saint, "is like striking flint with steel in order to start a fire. As soon as the spark has set the tinder ablaze, the flint is laid aside. Likewise, with reflections and considerations, we must strike the hard flint of our heart until it becomes inflamed with the love of God and the desire for humility, for mortification, for sufferings or for any other virtue. Once we have reached this point, we should stop there and try to take a firm hold on it, for without a doubt, this is the best prayer, more useful than many high reflections and sublime considerations.

✠

10. Those whose piety is not too solid go along happily and well when God gives them consolations in prayer. But if He deprives them of such delights, they immediately begin to languish discontentedly, just like children who thank their mother when she gives them sweets, but cry when she takes them away. Sensible spiritual consolations ordinarily generate complacency and this, in turn, begets pride, which poisons the soul and corrupts every good deed. For this reason, although at first Our Lord gives them to us in order to entice us, He afterwards deprives us of them to prevent them from harming us. *St. Francis de Sales*

St. John Berchmans frequently experienced great consolation in prayer, but every once in a while he also felt great aridity. However, he never was disheartened or saddened.

✠

11. When the soul finds itself oppressed by aridity, it must offer the prayer of reverence, confidence and conformity to God's will, remaining in the Lord's presence like a beggar before his king, uttering expressions of loving submission to His divine pleasure. *St. Jane Frances de Chantal*

St. Francis de Sales never worried about desolations, aridity and interior abandonment. He once told St. Jane Frances de Chantal that when he prayed it was not his custom to reflect on whether he was experiencing consolation or desolation. When God gave him good sentiments, he received them with profound reverence and simplicity. If he was not given them, he did not think of it at all. Rather he ever remained in God's presence with great confidence.

✠

12. He who wants to progress in prayer should not place much value on spiritual consolations, because I know from experience that the soul has advanced considerably who is truly determined to let it make no difference whether the Lord gives delights and signs of tender affection or denies them. *St. Teresa of Avila*

When St. John Berchmans was asked what steps he took to endure aridity, he replied, "I pray, keep myself busy and am patient."

✠

13. Another thing that may upset those who dedicate themselves to prayer is distractions which come during it. The mind is led astray and often with it the heart, too. Sometimes these dis-

tractions are caused by a lack of mortification of the senses, other times by the distracted state of the soul, and still more often they are permitted by the Lord to test His servants. Now, when bothered by distractions, one must call his thoughts back from time to time, stirring up his faith in the presence of God, and stay in that presence reverently and respectfully. If he cannot keep his mind on the appointed subject, he must bear these vexations and annoyances humbly and patiently.

St. Jane Frances de Chantal used to say to her Religious: "When you find yourself disturbed by distractions during prayer, it is wise to offer the prayer of patience, and, if you can, humbly and lovingly say, "Lord, You are the only support of my soul and my whole consolation."

St. John Chrysostom advised one who was easily carried away by distractions during prayer to arouse himself with this thought: "What! If I am chatting with a friend about the latest news, I give him my undivided attention. And now that I am talking with God about forgiveness of my sins and the way to save myself, I am sluggish and listless. My knees are bent but my mind is far away! Where is my faith? Where is the thought of the judgment?"

☩

14. The sole aim of whoever gives himself to prayer must be to prepare himself to the best of his

ability to conform his will to that of God. In this consists the greatest perfection that can be acquired in the spiritual life.
St. Teresa of Avila

The aim of all this Saint's prayers was precisely to conform herself in everything to the divine Will. This, also, was the goal St. Bernard set himself at the outset of his prayer, as we read in his life. He would always urge himself to pray with the desire of learning the will of God and doing it. We read the same of St. Vincent de Paul and many other Saints.

☩

15. Our prayer must be humble, fervent, resigned, persevering and deeply reverent, for we must reflect that we are in the presence of a God, and speaking with a Lord before Whom the Angels tremble out of respect and fear.
St. Mary Magdalene de Pazzi

Even when alone for the whole time he was at prayer, St. Francis de Sales would remain in the presence of God in a humble manner, motionless and with unusual reverence.

St. John Berchmans always prayed on his knees; with his hands folded at his breast, without leaning against the pew, motionless, such a serene, fervent expression on his face that many knelt near him to observe him and become more fervent themselves.

☩

16. Free yourself for a little while from your many cares, and take some time to think of God and to rest in Him. Enter into your heart and banish everything except your Creator and whatever can help you find Him. Then having shut the door, say with your whole soul: "Lord, I seek Your divine countenance; teach me how to find it again."
St. Augustine

St. Francis de Sales called the center of his soul God's Sanctuary, where no one but the soul and God enter. This was his retreat, his usual dwelling place. In his soul only purity, simplicity, humility and union with God were to be found.

When St. Bernard entered church to pray, he would say to his thoughts: "Stay outside, useless thoughts and disorderly affections, and you, my soul, enter into the judgment of your God."

☩

17. They who can shut themselves in the tiny heaven of the soul, where He Who created heaven and earth dwells, may be certain that in a short time they will progress far. *St. Teresa of Avila*

St. Catherine of Siena greatly loved retirement and, having been given many household duties and chores by

Prayer

her parents, she formed a cell in her own heart and there she remained continually united with God even when busiest, contemplating Him and speaking familiarly with Him. Thus she attained to a stable, uninterrupted union with her Lord.

"How helpful it is for me," said St. Teresa, "to remember that I have company within me—God!"

✠

18. When praying, we do not always have to reason with our minds. We may also remain in God's presence to discuss things with Him and find comfort in Him, without tiring ourselves by talking too much. We may simply point out our needs to Him and His obligation to have pity on us. For example, in considering an event of the Passion, it is good to pause there, and meditate on the sufferings our Savior underwent. However, the soul should not tire herself in a constant effort to do this. Rather let her remain there with Christ, and having quieted the intellect, if possible, occupy it with the thought that God is gazing upon her.   *St. Teresa of Avila*

Gersone tells us that a servant of God used to say: "For forty years I have been attending to prayer with all possible diligence, and I have not found a better or easier way to pray well than to present myself before God as a child, or as a poor beggar—blind, ragged and abandoned." St. Francis of Assisi must have done the same when he spent whole nights saying these few words: "My God, Who are You and who am I?" He would repeat them over and over, pondering on them and arousing within himself first love for a God so great and so good, and then contempt for himself as a low, ungrateful creature. In shame and confusion, at the thought of what he considered his many failings, he would beg God's pardon.

✠

19. In prayer, it is well, at times, to apply ourselves to praising and loving God, resolving to please Him in all things, rejoicing in His goodness and in His being what He is, desiring His greater honor and glory, recommending ourselves to His mercy. Or we may simply place ourselves before Him, contemplating His greatness and mercy and at the same time considering our own lowliness and misery. We then leave it up to Him to give us whatever He pleases, for He knows better than we what is good for us. *St. Teresa of Avila*

We read in the life of St. Jane Frances de Chantal that she found her delight in considering the infinite perfections of God and in desiring that this Supreme Good be known and loved by all His creatures.

Blessed Egidius, the companion of St. Francis, often meditated with great affection on the perfections of God and His gifts to men. Hence he made great progress in his love for God.

Prayer

✠

20. During mental prayer, it is well, at times, to imagine that many insults and injuries are being heaped upon us, that misfortunes have befallen us, and then strive to train our heart to forgive and bear these things patiently, in imitation of our Savior. This is the way to acquire a strong spirit.
St. Philip Neri

Once while ill, St. Ignatius set himself to determine whether there were anything which would be able to upset him. After considering many possible trials and misfortunes, he concluded that nothing would have the power to trouble him or destroy his peace except the breaking up of his Society. However, after meditating several times on this point he gained such control over himself that he said if it were to happen, after a quarter of an hour spent in prayer, he would be tranquil again.

✠

21. We must give great importance to meditation on the Passion of our Redeemer. Simply remembering or reflecting on the Passion is worth more than scourging one's self once a week for a year and fasting on bread and water, or reading the entire Psalter every day.   *St. Albert the Great*

From meditating for a long time on the Passion, the Empress Leonora conceived such a tender love for Jesus

Crucified that she said should she be sure of saving herself amidst riches and honors she would nevertheless choose the way of the cross in order to be like her Lord. For this reason she made light of her ills and sufferings, never complaining. And if someone showed sympathy for her, she would say: "This cross is very light and very dear to me. Without it I would not be happy."

✠

22. Just as one often visits a friend, wishing him good morning at the start of the day and good night at the close, and calls on him frequently in the hours between, so should you often visit Jesus in the Most Blessed Sacrament. In every visit offer His Most Precious Blood to the Eternal Father several times and you will find these visits marvelously increasing your love.   *St. Mary Magdalene de Pazzi*

St. Vincent de Paul used to visit Jesus in the Blessed Sacrament as frequently as possible. The only respite he took from his pressing duties were his long vigils before the Blessed Sacrament. His demeanor when kneeling there was so humble and his whole appearance so modest and devout that it seemed he actually beheld Jesus Christ in person.

✠

23. We must never forget to keep striving to know ourselves. This is most essential for progress

in prayer. But it must be done with moderation. I mean that after a soul has become convinced that of itself it possesses nothing good, and is filled with shame and confusion in the presence of so great a King, realizing how little it gives in return for all it owes, what need is there, then, to hold it back and, make it spend more time in this? It must be permitted to go to the consideration of other things which God places before it, so that forgetting itself it will fly to consider the wonders of its God.

St. Teresa of Avila

It is narrated that a young monk said to an older one. "Father, my reason tells me I am good." And the older one answered, "He who does not see his sins always thinks himself good. But he who sees his sins cannot be so persuaded. Hence the need to strive to know oneself."

✠

24. The great work of our perfection is born, grows, and thrives by means of two little but valuable practices: aspirations and spiritual retreats. Aspirations are transports of the spirit toward God. The more intense and loving they are, the better they are. Retreats are interior glances of the soul toward God. The simpler they are, the more worthwhile they are. A simple consideration is made of

Who God is and what He has done for us. Then the heart is moved to make acts of humility, love, resignation, confidence, and the like, according to the particular occasions. *St. Francis de Sales*

Every time the hour struck, St. Ignatius would withdraw within himself and raise his mind to God. Likewise at each stroke of the hour, St. Vincent de Paul would remove his hat and recite an aspiration, even when in the company of very important persons.

✠

25. It requires great humility to accustom one's self to make of everything a subject for reflection in order to rise from these things to God, contemplating in them His perfections and His love for us as well as our obligation to serve Him faithfully.

Scupoli

This was habitual with St. Francis de Sales. At the sight of beautiful fields, he used to say, "We are the fields cultivated by God." Magnificent and beautifully decorated churches would cause him to exclaim: "We are the living temples of God, and why are souls not so beautifully adorned with virtues?" Upon seeing flowers: "When will our flowers bear fruit?" On contemplating rare and precious works of art: "There is nothing more beautiful than a soul made to the image and likeness of God." Thus everything he beheld served to lift his mind to God.

26. There is a certain way of praying which is very easy and very beneficial. It consists in accustoming our soul to God's presence, but in such a way as to produce in us an intimate, simple and perfect union. Oh, what a precious prayer this is!
St. Francis de Sales

For St. Aloysius Gonzaga nothing was easier than to keep his mind continuously united to God. In fact, he found it as difficult to tear his thoughts from God as others do to keep united to God.

✠

27. If for one year we have faithfully walked in God's presence, at the end of that time we shall have reached the heights of perfection without having noticed it. *St. Teresa of Avila*

It is narrated in the lives of the Fathers of the desert that a holy Abbot advised one of his Novices never to lose sight of God, remembering that He is ever-present. This is the method of all methods, the one God taught Abraham when He said: "Walk in My presence and you will be perfect."

✠

28. The majority of the faults committed by Religious against their Rules and all their practices

of piety stem from the fact that they easily lose the sense of God's presence.   *St. Francis de Sales*

Of St. John Berchmans it is said that he never lost sight of the presence of God, and that this practice came unusually easy and natural to him. Yet he was always present to himself and to what he was doing and exact in his dealings with all. Because he lived in the presence of God he fulfilled his spiritual practices with great devotion and was never known to transgress the least Rule or commit the smallest defect.

☧

29. There is a certain way of living in the presence of God through which, if the soul so desires, it can remain always in prayer and continually aflame with love of God. It is realized by carrying out one's duties with the thought of doing God's will, and taking delight in that.   *St. Alphonsus Rodriguez*

Many years before his death, St. Francis de Sales found himself so taken up by many duties that he hardly found time for his prayer. When St. Jane Frances de Chantal asked one day whether he had prayed, he answered: "No, but I did the equivalent." In other words, he did his best to be continually united to God. He was wont to say that in this way his was a prayer of work and action. Thus his life was a continual prayer. He was not content to enjoy only a delightful union with God during prayer, but loved His will equally well.

Prayer

✠

30. The highest and most perfect prayer is contemplation. But this is entirely the work of God, since contemplation is supernatural and superior to our nature. Hence in this type of prayer the soul can do nothing. It can only prepare itself for it. Now, the best preparation is to be humble, to try sincerely to acquire virtue, especially fraternal charity and love of God, have a firm resolve to do God's will in all things, walk along the way of the cross and extinguish self-love. *St. Teresa of Avila*

When St. Augustine the Abbot was asked how he could spend entire nights in prayer, he answered: "I never knew what true contemplation was while I was concerned about myself. But when I succeeded in ridding my mind of all restless thoughts and detaching my heart from all earthly affection, I began to taste that admirable fruit of the divine will which purified souls customarily enjoy in contemplation."

A very enlightened soul wrote thus: "Through experience I have found that to learn mystical theology one must study the crucifix more than books. I mean that one must strive to practice virtue by imitating Jesus Christ and attending to purity of life, prayer, and constancy in doing and suffering whatever God wants of us."

OCTOBER

Confidence

Behold, I am with you.
Matt. 28:20

1. As God is infinite omnipotence, nothing is impossible to Him; as infinite wisdom, nothing is difficult to Him; as goodness without measure, He has an infinite concern for our welfare. Now, should not all this suffice to make us place all our confidence in Him? *Scupoli*

Our Lord once said to St. Gertrude: "The firm confidence a person has in Me, believing that I truly can help him at all times and desire to do so, steals My Heart and does such violence to Me, that I cannot but favor such a soul because of the great pleasure I experience in seeing it so dependent upon Me and in order to satisfy the great love I have for it."

☨

2. God certainly desires our greatest good, more than we ourselves do. Better than we He knows how it can be effected. The choice of these means is entirely in His hands, since it is He Who disposes and regulates all that happens in this

world. It is therefore absolutely certain that whatever befalls us, will always be the best for us.

St. Augustine

Knowing that whatever happens, great or small, happens by order or permission of Divine Providence, St. Francis de Sales used to entrust himself to it even more than a child does upon his mother's knee. He was wont to say that God had taught him this lesson from his childhood, and that if he were to be born again, he would despise human prudence more than ever and would permit himself to be ruled entirely by God.

☩

3. Do you want proof that whatever happens is for our good? This is it. God has said: "I will never abandon you; I will be with you always." If a gentleman should promise you this, you would trust him. God makes this promise to you, and do you doubt it? Do you want a stronger foundation for belief than the word of God, which is infallible? Yes, He promised it, He wrote it, He has given His word, so rest assured. *St. Augustine*

We read in the life of St. Rose of Lima that she had inherited her mother's natural timidity and fear, and hence would not even go from one room to another in the dark without a light, except to pray. When it came to that, she would overcome all her fears. One night she remained at prayer longer than usual in a hut she had built for herself in the garden. Her mother, fearing that something had happened to her, wanted to go to call her. However, being afraid of the dark, she asked her husband to go with her. When Rose saw them, she stood up and went back to the house with them, excusing herself for her tardiness. On the way, she thought to herself: "Look! My mother is as afraid of the dark as I am, but with her husband, she feels secure. And I, with my Spouse, Who is always at my side and in my heart, should I be afraid?" This reflection made such an impression on her that her fear vanished, and from that time on she was never afraid of anything.

☩

4. We are convinced beyond doubt that the truths of faith cannot deceive us; yet we cannot seem to bring ourselves to trust in them. It is easier for us to trust in human reasons and the deceiving appearances of the world. This, precisely, is the reason for our poor progress in virtue and in all that pertains to God's glory.   *St. Vincent de Paul*

St. Anthony and St. Francis reached such a high degree of perfection because they went by the words of the Gospel: "If you wish to be perfect, go, sell what you have, give it to the poor, and come, follow Me."

☩

5. It is absolutely necessary for our own good and the good of others to accustom ourselves to

Confidence

follow in all things the light of faith, which brings a certain devotion that it diffuses in the hearts of men. Yes, only eternal truth can fill our hearts and lead us along the right road. Believe me, it is enough to establish oneself firmly on these divine foundations in order to reach perfection and do great things in a short time. *St. Vincent de Paul*

One winter day St. Francis' brother saw the saint barefoot, poorly dressed and trembling with cold, so he sent a boy to ask the saint mockingly in his name if he wished to sell him a drop of his perspiration. Joyfully the saint answered: "Tell my brother that I have already sold it all to my Lord and my God, and at a very good price."

✠

6. O God of my soul, who can adequately express what You give to those who confide in You, and what they lose who, having had ecstasies, trust in themselves. *St. Teresa of Avila*

St. Teresa said she had known persons outstanding for virtue, who had attained the prayer of union, and yet were later conquered by the devil. The reason for this could have been that they trusted too much in themselves. In fact, seeing itself so close to God, knowing the difference between the goods of Heaven and those of earth, and experiencing the evidence of God's great love for it, the soul consequently feels sure that it will never fall from its enjoyment of such a treasure. It cannot even understand how so delightful a life could be exchanged for base sensual pleasures. Thus confident, the soul begins to place itself in occasions and to fall into sin, not realizing that it is still incapable of leaving the nest and flying, that as yet it is neither well established in virtues nor experienced enough to recognize the dangers.

✠

7. To trust in one's own talents is extremely harmful. When a superior, for example, or a preacher or a confessor puts his confidence in his own prudence, learning and spirit, to make him realize his insufficiency, God removes His help and leaves him on his own. Consequently, all his labors and efforts produce little or no results. This is the reason why we frequently do not succeed in our undertakings. *St. Vincent de Paul*

St. Francis de Sales was always successful in every task God entrusted to him. The explanation of his success was that he did not trust in his ability but relied entirely on Divine Providence. Moreover, he never entertained greater hopes of succeeding than when he had no other help than this.

St. Philip Neri was wont to say: "When a person places himself in the occasion of sin and says: 'I will not fall, I will not commit that sin,' it is an almost sure sign that he will commit it, with greater harm to his soul."

✠

8. Let us strive to develop a strong distrust of ourselves and to become firmly convinced that of ourselves we are incapable of doing anything but spoil God's plans. This lowly concept of ourselves will keep us completely dependent upon God and lead us to have constant recourse to Him.
St. Vincent de Paul

The Venerable Father Daponte used to say that what made others discouraged, such as their human frailty, weakness and sins, made him even more confident, because he kept his gaze unswervingly fixed on God's goodness and mercy.

St. Philip Neri would frequently address God thus: "Lord, do not trust me, because if You do not help me, I shall surely fall."

✠

9. Take care not to depend upon or give too much importance to the friendship and support of men, because they alone cannot sustain us, and when God sees us depending on them, He withdraws.
St. Vincent de Paul

St. Teresa said one day: "Now I clearly understand that one cannot rest secure if he places his trust in men, for at the least contradiction or complaint they turn away from you. Our true friend, Whom alone we can trust, is Jesus

Christ. When I depend upon Him, I feel so strong that I think I could stand firm against the whole world."

☨

10. Whoever handles matters by means of deceit and subterfuges offends the Providence of God and renders himself unworthy of His paternal care.
St. Vincent de Paul

In all he said and did, this glorious saint made it clear that he was extremely averse to all forms of pretense and left clever deceits to the worldly wise.

The same may be said of St. Bonaventure, St. Thomas, St. Charles, St. Mary Magdalene de Pazzi and others. All of them were very successful in their undertakings and as a result were greatly esteemed and favored not only by God but also by men.

☨

11. When one thinks only of God, and confides entirely in Him, trying to serve Him faithfully, God takes care of him. The greater the confidence placed in Him, the greater His care. Nor is there any danger of His care failing, since He has an infinite love for those who trust in Him. *St. Francis de Sales*

One day Our Lord said to St. Catherine of Siena: "Think of Me and I will think of you. I will take complete care of everything that pertains to you."

St. Hugo tells us that the more he attended to the worship of God with all care and diligence, the more God provided him with the necessities of life.

Taulero relates that a certain servant of God frequently was asked by various persons to pray for their special intentions. She would promise to pray, but then at times forget to do so. Yet those people always received the graces they asked for and returned to thank her for her prayers. Surprised, she asked God one day: "How is it, Lord, that You grant these graces without my asking for them?" And the Lord replied: "You see, My daughter, the day you gave Me your will, I gave you Mine. Hence, even when at times you do not ask Me for anything in particular, since I know you would like it, I grant it just as though you had asked Me for it."

✠

12. He who serves God with a pure heart and, with no thought to any personal and human interest, seeks God's glory alone, must always hope for the successful outcome of his enterprises, especially when, according to human judgment, there seems to be no hope. For efforts made in the service of God are over and above human prudence and depend upon a higher principle. *St. Charles Borromeo*

The holy Cardinal had recourse to God for everything in prayer. He would begin, continue and finish his every action with prayer. The more difficult and important his undertakings, the more he would pray. At times, when matters were not only difficult but even desperate, he would not cease to pray on that account or give up. Rather he would go ahead with greater effort and more frequent prayer. For this reason he succeeded in many and great things, which appeared humanly impossible.

⸙

13. It is in times of grave necessity that we can find out whether we really trust in God. Believe me, three workers do more than ten when God has a hand in things. And He takes a hand when He removes human means and places us in the need of doing things beyond our capability.

St. Vincent de Paul

Upon being told by the Procurator of the house that they did not have a cent for the usual expenses and for the extra expenses of the coming Ordination, St. Vincent de Paul tranquilly and cheerfully answered, with full confidence in God, "Oh, what good news this is! May God be praised. Now is the time to show that we trust in Him. The treasures of Providence are infinite and our lack of confidence is an insult to God."

When attacked by a great multitude of his enemies, King Josaphat said to his men: "We cannot hold our own against so many, so let us raise our eyes to God and trust in Him, and everything will go well with us." And indeed it did.

✠

14. When we must undertake some work in the service of God, after having asked Him to enlighten us and having recognized His will, even if we consider it necessary and opportune to make use of human means, we must not place our confidence in them but solely in the divine assistance.
St. Vincent de Paul

In all his undertakings, St. Ignatius Loyola worked as though everything depended entirely on himself and placed all his trust in God, as though everything depended on God.

✠

15. It is from divine assistance that we must expect the successful outcome of our work, firmly convinced that whatever happens will always be the best for us regardless of whether in our opinion it seems good or bad. *St. Vincent de Paul*

One day, when someone recommended himself to St. Vincent's prayers, he answered: "I have been engrossed in various affairs all morning and have been able to say only a few prayers, and these with many distractions. Hence, judge for yourself what you can hope for from my prayers. However, this does not discourage me, because I place all my trust in God, certain that the throne of God's goodness and mercy is erected on the foundation of our miseries."

✠

16. In taking care of our daily affairs and needs we must not be carried away by worries. We should take reasonable moderate care, and then leave everything up to the dispositions and charge of Divine Providence, letting God direct all things to their proper end and manifest His will to us. Let us rest assured that when God wants an affair to succeed, delay will do no harm and furthermore, the less there is of what is ours in the matter, the more there will be of the divine.

St. Vincent de Paul

The ordinary practice of this saint was to have recourse to supernatural means before using human means. He would recommend the matter to God and then calmly wait for Him to begin it according to His plans and for His greater glory.

✠

17. Our frantic concern to find out ways and means of arming ourselves against the events and trials of this life is a great lack of confidence in God. Forestalling in this manner the dispositions of Divine Providence we show that we trust more in our own efforts than in God's holy ways and that we rely more on human prudence than on His promises.

St. Vincent de Paul

Confidence

When Father Alvarez was the rector of a poor college, he had an assistant who would often tell him anxiously and concernedly about their current needs and about the necessity of considering the state of the college. Father Alvarez would ask him whether he had recommended it to God, and upon the latter's answering that he did not have time to pray, Father Alvarez would say, "But that is the first thing to do. Why don't you go pray a while to the Lord. Surely you don't think that this flock is without a Shepherd Who takes their life to heart? Do go in peace and remember that it does not depend on your efforts."

✠

18. Once the will of God in some matter is known, no matter how hard it may be, it should be undertaken fearlessly and brought to completion regardless of how many or how great be the obstacles encountered. Divine Providence never fails in matters undertaken for His love.   *St. Vincent de Paul*

After having given prudent, mature thought to a possible undertaking and judged it good for the service of God, St. Charles would begin it and courageously bring it to successful completion, although to others it seemed impossible.

Whenever St. Francis Xavier spied an opportunity to give glory to God, he lost no time in making the most of it without fearing either difficulties or dangers.

✠

19. Let us place our confidence in God and set ourselves in complete dependence upon His Providence. Then we need not worry about what others say of us or do to us, for it will all turn out to our advantage. *St. Vincent de Paul*

One night St. Gregory Bishop of Agrigento went to chapel to recite matins. While he was praying, some enemies had a woman go to his room. Then, after matins, they insisted on accompanying him to his room. When the woman saw them, she began to scream, as they had arranged beforehand, and accused the holy bishop of sacrilege. As a result, his reputation was ruined and he was condemned by the Pope. But God took care of him. Saints Peter and Paul appeared to him and consoled him. At the same time, the woman became possessed by the devil and was greatly tormented by him until she appeared at a Bishops' council and revealed the entire plot. Then she was healed by the saint. The evil men were condemned to severe punishment and the saint was absolved by the Pope and the fame of his holiness spread far and wide.

✠

20. When calumniated, weak souls, too attached to their reputation, immediately raise a hue and cry and give themselves no peace. But this is not the case with generous souls who seek only to please God. They well know that God sees their

innocence and that it is dearer to Him than to them and that therefore He will not fail to defend it.

St. Augustine

St. Francis de Sales wrote to Monsignor Camus: "From Paris I have been notified that I am being criticized. However, I hope that the good Lord will adjust matters better than they were before, if such should be necessary for His service. For my part, I only want the reputation necessary for this. As long as God is served, what does it matter whether we do it with a good or bad reputation, with praise or criticism? May He dispose of my name and honor as He pleases."

✠

21. When one places all his confidence in God, God protects him in a special way at all times, and thus he can rest assured that nothing evil will befall him. *St. Vincent de Paul*

Overhearing someone talking about current troubles, Emperor Ferdinand II said: "Let us do our part and then leave everything—ourselves and our affairs—up to God. He will take good care of everything." When speaking of a possible calamity, he would say: "God will provide."

✠

22. After we have placed ourselves entirely in God's hands with complete confidence in Him,

we must not fear any adversity; for if some misfortune should befall us, God will know how to turn it to our good through ways which we do not know now but will know some day. *St. Vincent de Paul*

Returning from a visit to the Holy Land, St. Ignatius arrived at Cypress and found there three ships ready to sail for Italy. The first belonged to the Turks. The second was a large, strong and well-armed Venetian ship. The third was a small, old and worm-eaten vessel. Many begged the captain of the Venetian ship to take Ignatius on board for the love of God. They praised him and said he was a saint. But upon hearing that Ignatius was poor and would be unable to pay his passage, the captain answered that if he were a saint, he did not need a ship but could walk over the sea as other saints had done. Hence Ignatius was forced to beg passage on the old ship. There he was warmly received. The three ships set out on the same day with favorable winds and made good time. Towards evening a storm broke out. The Turkish vessel and all its passengers sank. The Venetian ship was dashed against a sand bank and it passengers just barely escaped death. Only the old ship reached port safely.

✠

23. When we find ourselves in some grave danger we must not lose courage but firmly trust in God, for where there is the greatest danger, there is also the greatest help from Him Who wants to be called our *"Help"* in times of peace and in times of tribulation. *St. Ambrose*

Confidence 219

When his ship was caught in a great storm at sea, St. Ignatius of Loyola was the only one on board who was not moaning and trembling in fear of death. He was cheerful and unafraid, in fact, reflecting that without God's permission storms cannot come up or death take anyone.

✠

24. There are some whose confidence in God is so strong that they cannot abandon it even in extreme or desperate cases. Oh, how dear to God are those souls, and how much He helps them!

Although Emperor Ferdinand II saw his enemies leagued against him and his lands devastated, he never lost confidence in God, but always said: "God will see me safely through this storm." Nor was he disappointed, because when his cause seemed most desperate he won a great victory over all his enemies.

What case was more desperate than Susanna's? Falsely accused, condemned and led to her death, she still trusted in God and was freed.

✠

25. He who does not lose heart when faced with unforeseen adversities but immediately turns to God with confidence gives evidence of being well rooted in this virtue. *St. Alphonsus Rodriguez*

We read in the lives of the holy Fathers of the desert that one day St. Colombanus found himself surrounded by twelve wolves. Clawing at his clothes, they made ready to tear him to pieces. Without becoming excited, he invoked God's help with great confidence, saying: "Incline unto my aid, O God. O Lord, make haste to help me." At these words the wolves fled.

✠

26. Christian confidence consists in perfect abandonment in God over and above every provision of human prudence. Oh, what joy it is to walk in this perfect dependence on Providence, to be always under this divine protection!

St. Jane Frances de Chantal

Such was Abraham's confidence. He hoped that his descendants would spread throughout the entire world, as God had promised him, even though he had been ordered by God to sacrifice his only son when he was too old to have other children.

Such, also, was the faith of holy Job. Afflicted in body, his children and wealth taken from him, derided by his friends, he said: "Although God should kill me, I will always hope in Him."

✠

27. He who places himself entirely in the arms of Divine Providence and lets himself be carried

Confidence

by God, travels in a carriage, so to speak, and hardly feels the weight of his crosses. He who does the opposite goes on foot, dragging his crosses weariedly and painfully.
St. Bernard

There once lived a poor young girl who was confined to her bed and suffered greatly. Yet, whoever went to visit her, found her always happy. When asked how she could be so cheerful amid such suffering, she replied that she thought only of God and lived like a little bird under the wings of Divine Providence. Hence she was neither afraid nor upset.

☩

28. The servant of God must not fear anything. He must not even pay much attention to the demons. For when they are disregarded, they are powerless. If God is powerful and the demons are His slaves, what harm can they do to those who are the servants of so great a King and Lord?
St. Teresa of Avila

The same saint attests that she was timid by nature and often did not even dare to stay alone in a room in broad daylight. One day, upon reflecting how inconvenient it is to be fearful and timid while we have such a powerful God Who rules everything, she said to herself: "What do I fear? Whom do I fear?" And taking a crucifix in her hand she began to defy the demons, saying: "Come, all of you. I am the servant of God, so I want to see what you can do to me." After that, she felt full of courage and all her fears vanished.

✠

29. No matter how many sins, even serious ones, and imperfections one may have committed and commits, he must never despair of salvation, nor lose confidence in God. The divine clemency is infinitely greater than human malice.

St. John Chrysostom

St. Vincent Ferrer's confidence in God was admirable. One day he was told of a dying man who was in despair because of his grave sins and refused to confess himself. St. Vincent hurried to him, confident that he would win him to repentance. Reaching his side, he said: "Brother, knowing that Jesus Christ died for you, why do you want to despair of His mercy? This is a great insult to the immense goodness He has shown you." The sick man, greatly angered by these words, answered: "It is precisely for this reason that I want to damn myself, to spite Christ." "In spite of yourself you will be saved!" cried the saint. Then turning to the bystanders he said: "Let us recite the Rosary to ask the Blessed Virgin Mary for the conversion of this most obstinate sinner." And God willed to manifest His pleasure at the generous confidence of His servant, for before the recitation of the Rosary was over, the room was filled with a bright light and the great Mother of God appeared holding the divine Babe, Who was covered with blood. At this sight the sinner's heart melted with compunction. He confessed his sins with great sorrow and shortly afterwards yielded his soul to God.

Confidence

✠

30-31. If we want to perform our duties well and provide for all our needs, we must look up to God every once in a while—like navigators, who look up at the stars in order to keep on the right course more than at the sea on which they are sailing.

NOVEMBER

Charity

> *This is the greatest and the first commandment. You shall love the Lord your God with your whole heart, with your whole soul and with your whole mind. And the second is like it: You shall love your neighbor as yourself.*
>
> Matt. 22:37-38

1. My Lord and my God, what need was there for You to give me the precept to love you? Are You not most lovable for Your infinite perfections? And for the infinite love You bear us, do You not deserve our love? Now, how could there be anyone who does not love You? If there is, it is because he does not merit to know You. A soul who knows God cannot help but love Him and love Him in proportion to the knowledge he has of Him. Hence if he has little love for Him it is because he does not know Him well. The more he grows in knowledge of God, the more his love for Him will increase.

St. Teresa of Avila

Blessed Jacapone could not bear to see people giving themselves over to sin, especially during the days of Mardi Gras, and he would repeat: "Love is not loved! Love is not loved because He is not known." and St. Philip would say: "Lord, I do not love You because I do not know You."

✠

2. When one has reached the point of resting his heart totally in God, he loses his affection for all things. He no longer finds consolation in anything save God, and of nothing does he feel so sure as of God. His own honor and his own interests are completely forgotten. *St. Teresa of Avila*

"When some created thing comforts and delights me, I do not dare declare that my love for God is ardent," St. Bernard used to say.

St. Ignatius Loyola arrived at such a degree, that he had lost affection for all things and had nothing else in his heart but the desire to please God and win His affection.

✠

3. Alas! We do not have as much love as we should have. I mean to say that our love would have to be infinite in order to have enough with which to love our God. Yet miserable creatures that we are, we squander it on vile and empty things as though we had it to spare. *St. Francis de Sales*

This great saint once said: "If I knew that only one fiber of affection in my soul were not of God and for God, I would tear it out immediately. I would prefer to be nothing at all rather than not entirely of God."

Frequently St. Philip Neri would cry out, "How is it possible that one who believes in God can love others?" And, complaining to God he would exclaim: "O Lord, You Who are so amiable and have commanded that I love You, why have You given me but one heart, and such a small one at that?"

✠

4. When a soul that really loves God knows that a thing is of greater perfection and service to Him, she does it at once and without difficulty, because of the joy she feels in pleasing Him. Oh, my God! We must really love You and leave everything for love of You, so that You may make all things easy. *St. Teresa of Avila*

It is well known that St. Ignatius Loyola sought nothing but the glory of God—the greatest glory possible, moreover. In the Collect prescribed for the saint's Mass, the Church gives as his distinctive characteristic his election by God to propagate His greater glory.

✠

5. When the love of God has taken possession of a soul, it produces an insatiable yearning to work for the beloved—so much so, that no matter how much is done and no matter how much time is spent in His service, it all seems nothing and the

soul is always distressed over having done too little for his God. And if it were permissible to do away with himself and die for Him, he would be greatly consoled. *St. John Chrysostom*

St. Charles was outstanding in his love of God. As long as he lived he had an insatiable desire to honor Him, to promote and spread worship of Him. This desire spurred him on to work unweariningly. In fact, he seemed more refreshed than ever as one tiresome task followed another without interruption. While his co-workers frequently were overcome with exhaustion he never even seemed to feel the least bit of fatigue, almost as though work were recreation and relaxation for him. What is more, with all his great accomplishments in the service of his God, he was never satisfied with what he had done. He continually sought new ways of doing things and never did he think or speak of anything but God and what pertained to His honor and service.

✠

6. When one has attained to perfect love of God he lives as though alone in the world. He no longer cares about glory or ignominy; he scorns temptations and sufferings and loses his taste for all things. Finding no help, consolation or rest in anything, he incessantly seeks his beloved, without ever tiring. *St. John Chrysostom*

This was St. Vincent Ferrer's way of life. It is written of him that his heart and mind were always full of God and that he only spoke of God and with God.

7. The perfect love of God does not consist in delights, tears and sentiments of devotion that we generally desire. It consists, rather, in a strong determination and burning desire to please God in all things and in the effort to avoid offending Him as far as possible and to promote His glory.

St. Teresa of Avila

Saint Jane Frances de Chantal understood this fact very well. Upon hearing that one of her Religious was considered a great lover of God because she enjoyed extraordinary consolations, Mother de Chantal wrote to the Sister's Superior: "This good Sister is much in need of being made to see her error. She thinks herself quite advanced in the love of God, yet she is not as much advanced in virtue. I believe that those ardent feelings she experiences are but the products of nature and self-love. Hence, for her own good she must be taught that true, solid love does not consist in experiencing divine sweetness, but rather in the exact observance of the Rule and the faithful practice of virtue; that is, in self-humiliation, in loving to be despised, in bearing injuries and adversities, in forgetting one's self, and in a love that does not care to be known except by God."

8. The love of God is the tree of life in the middle of the earthly paradise. Like all other trees it has six parts: roots, trunk, branches, leaves, flowers and fruits. The roots are the virtues, by means of which love is acquired. The trunk is the

yielding of our will to the will of God. The branches are contained in these words: *I sat under the shade of Him Whom I had desired.* The first of these is faith; the second, true confidence in the divine protection; the third, the ardent desires, firm resolutions and other interior acts which the soul continually makes to attain to true love; the fourth, the constancy with which she remains seated under this tree. The leaves are: 1. the new graces freely given; 2. the interior delights, joys, spiritual happiness, tenderness, tears, etc.; 3. ecstasies. The flowers are the works and the heroic virtues which the enamored soul produces. The fruits are the troubles, afflictions and persecutions which the soul bears with patience when God sends them or she herself seeks them in order to serve Him better and imitate the sufferings of Jesus Christ. *St. Teresa of Avila*

It is not surprising that this saint knew so well how to describe this tree, for she kept it deep rooted in her heart and well adorned in all its parts.

✠

9. Some torment themselves seeking ways of discovering the art of loving God. These poor souls do not know that there is no method or way of loving Him other than doing what is pleasing to Him.
St. Francis de Sales

St. Vincent de Paul excelled in this holy practice, doing God's will with great precision. He always kept a close watch on himself, checked his passions, reasoned rightly, spoke circumspectly, acted prudently, performed his practices of piety punctually, and was from all appearances so perfectly united to God that it was clear that the love of God animated his heart and ruled his every move and act. It may be said that his whole life was a continuous sacrifice to God, not only of the honors, comforts, pleasures and all the other goods of this world but still more of what he had received from God, such as enlightenment, affections, and desires.

✠

10. Love of God is acquired by resolving to work and suffer for God and to abstain from all that displeases Him when the temptations arise. The better to do this in great things one must grow accustomed to it in little things. *St. Teresa of Avila*

Outstanding in this virtue was St. Vincent de Paul. Because he would not consent to the smallest act against justice, simplicity and charity, he had to suffer harsh retorts, indiscreet questioning, reproofs, insults, wearying insistence, and other annoyances and offences. Yet, in none of these cases was he ever known to evidence impatience or utter a word of complaint.

✠

11. An excellent way to practice love of Jesus Christ is to grow accustomed to keeping Him always

present to our minds. This can be done in three ways: 1. Before performing an action, imagine how and with what spirit and intention He would do it, in order to imitate Him. 2. Think of Him ever gazing down on us from Heaven and showering us with His graces and counsels in abundance. 3. See Him in our neighbor. In this way all our actions will be performed with greater ease and perfection.
St. Vincent de Paul

This Saint practiced what he preached to the point of becoming outstanding in love of Christ. He never undertook anything, gave advice or performed any action without first fixing his mind's eye on the examples and teachings of Jesus Christ and on the reward He holds in readiness and distributes liberally to those who do good. He always saw Christ in his neighbor. Frequently he would say: "Christ said this, Christ did that...." And: "We must see Christ Himself in everyone."

✠

12. Do you want to know how you stand in the love of God? Here is your gauge: the more the soul grows in divine love, the greater is its desire to suffer and to be humiliated. This is the sure sign of the sacred flame; the rest is all smoke.
St. Vincent de Paul

St. John of the Cross showed how convinced he was of this fact. One day Jesus appeared to him and asked him what he wanted in return for all the trials and labors he had undergone for love of Him. "Lord," answered the saint, "I want nothing but to suffer and to be despised for Your sake."

☖

13. The true sign of loving nothing but God is loving Him equally at all times. Since He is always the same, the inequality of our love for Him can only spring from the consideration of something which is not Him. *St. Francis de Sales*

The holy Mother de Chantal was a living example of this perfect love of God. She was as content in times of desolation as in times of consolation although she had to suffer greatly from desolation for a long time. The reason for her constancy was, as she herself said, that she sought nothing else in joys and sorrows alike but the fulfillment of the divine will.

A saint once said that the true lovers of God are like the sun. Though at times it is hidden by clouds, its radiance and heat are always the same.

☖

14. The measure of one's charity is his lack of desires. As a soul's desires decrease, its charity increases. When it no longer feels any desires, it possesses perfect charity. *St. Augustine*

Charity

St. Francis de Sales used to say: "I want few things and the things I want I have very little desire for. I have almost no desires, in fact, and if I were to be born again I would not want any."

St. Teresa of Avila was quite persuaded of this truth. She would exclaim: "O Love, You love me more than I could love myself and more than I can understand! Why then, O Lord, should I desire more than what You want to give me?"

✠

15. The surest way to determine whether one possesses love of God is to see whether he loves his neighbor. These two loves are never separated. Rest assured, the more you progress in love of neighbor the more your love of God will increase. The best way to measure your love of God is to see how much you love your neighbor.

St. Teresa of Avila

St. Jerome relates that when St. John had reached an advanced age and was no longer able to take an active part in the sacred functions, unless supported by his disciples, or to give long sermons due to his weakened voice, he would repeatedly urge, "Little children, love one another." Weary of the same few words, his hearers asked him why he always preached thus to them. "Because," he answered, "this is the Lord's precept, and if you observe it, that alone is enough."

☩

16. We must reflect that not only did God recommend that we love our neighbor, but also prescribed *how* we should love him; that is, we must love him as ourself. This is the rule that cannot be transgressed without fault; and it is so essential to the love of neighbor, that if it were different it would not be sufficient.

Tertullian relates that the first Christians showed their love for one another with such expressive signs of affection that the pagans marvelled and said to one another: "See how these Christians love one another, how respectful they are to one another, how quick to offer their services to each other and how ready even to die for one another."

☩

17. Fraternal charity is a sign of predestination, because it distinguishes us as true disciples of Christ, since it was this divine virtue which moved Him to lead a life of poverty and to die naked on a cross. Hence, when we have occasion to suffer for charity, we must bless God. *St. Vincent de Paul*

St. Euphrasia, a Sister, was so inclined to be charitable that she often went without eating, so engrossed was she in her works of charity. So dear did she render herself to all her Sisters that they considered her more an angel than a creature of this earth. When Our Lord revealed to the Abbess that Euphrasia was to die soon, the latter, upon being informed, grieved that she would no longer be able to serve God in her neighbor.

18. God so loves our neighbor that He went so far as to give His life for him, and He is pleased when we leave Him to do good to our neighbor. How much, then, must the services we render our neighbor be pleasing to Him? If we could only realize how important is this virtue of love of neighbor, we would be concerned about nothing else.
St. Teresa of Avila

One morning before Communion, St. Gertrude was very sad because she could not go to confession to cleanse her soul of some of her imperfections. Our Lord consoled her by letting her see her soul adorned with many precious stones. "Why are you so sad," He said to her, "since you possess the virtue of charity which you well know covers a multitude of sins?"

St. Mary Magdalene de Pazzi so esteemed the virtue of charity that she considered lost the day she did not perform some act of charity toward her neighbor.

19. Oh, how great must be the love of the Son of God for the poor! He chose to be poor, He willed to be called the teacher of the poor, and in a special way considers as done to Himself all that is done for His poor. *St. Vincent de Paul*

This saint loved everyone, but the poor above all. For them he had a love that was more than fatherly. When he saw or heard of someone in need, his heart would at once fill with compassion and without being asked, he would think of how to provide for him. His main care and worry, in fact, was to help the needy and relieve the poor. While speaking one day about the bad weather which threatened to bring on a terrible famine, he sighed and said: "I am distressed not so much for our Congregation as for the poor! What will the poor do? Where will they go? To tell the truth, this is my greatest worry."

✠

20. The poor must be loved with a completely special affection. In them we must see Jesus Christ Himself and have as much care for them as He did.
St. Vincent de Paul

When he became a Bishop, Venerable de Palafox gave a dinner every Thursday to twelve poor people. He himself waited on them. Then, in reading the life of St. Martin, he found that this saint not only served the poor but even washed their feet. The holy bishop decided to do likewise. He performed all these services with as much satisfaction and attention as if he had been waiting on Jesus Christ Himself. This produced in him a great respect for the poor, and each time he met a needy person he seemed to see God Himself.

✠

21. Visiting and relieving the sick is most certainly pleasing to God, for He greatly recommended it. However, to practice this charity more willingly and more meritoriously, one must not look upon the sick person as an ordinary man, but as Christ Himself, Who declared that He receives that kindness as done to Himself.

St. Mary Magdalene de Pazzi's charity to the sick was incredible. Every day she visited them, and the most needy or seriously ill she visited several times daily. She would stay as long as they needed her, serving them in all their needs and either providing for them herself or having the superior do so. She encouraged them to eat, even tasting the food herself first. She straightened their beds, swept their rooms, read to them from spiritual books, exhorted them to be patient, and consoled them. All this she did with such joy and love that to all she was of great comfort.

✠

22. To love our neighbor as our Lord commanded, we must be good and warm-hearted, particularly when we find someone unattractive because of some natural or moral defect. Then, finding nothing in him to love for himself, we shall love him only for love of our Savior. The teaching of the saints is that in loving and doing good, we

should never consider the recipient, but rather the One for whose love we are acting.

St. Francis de Sales

St. Jane Frances de Chantal possessed this love of neighbor in a high degree. We read in her life that she never failed to show it plainly toward everyone, no matter what faults she might see in a person. Frequently she would exhort her Sisters thus: "We must bear with our poor, weak neighbor, as we find him, with his idiosyncrasies, and foolishness, his annoying changes of mood and little demands on our time and patience, his faults and thoughtlessness in our regard. These things do us no harm; they are just annoying. After all, we must have something to suffer."

☩

23. Let us refrain from complaining, nursing a grudge, or speaking evil of those who obviously dislike us, oppose our plans and advancement, or even persecute us with injuries, injustice and calumnies. Let us continue to treat them as well as always, or even better, and if we can, show them respect, speak well of them, do good to them, serve them in their needs and, if necessary, even accept humiliation and contempt in order to save their honor.

St. Vincent de Paul

That is precisely the way St. Vincent treated those who offended him. Not only did he willingly forgive and when necessary even obtain pardon for them from the authorities, but what is more, he compassionated and excused them. He continued to have respect for them and to show it, as though nothing had ever happened, doing all he could for them. Since he was most delicate in this matter of brotherly love, he did his utmost to rid them of the roots of rancor and to win their affection.

✠

24. Let us strive to have great compassion for weak and sinful souls, because he who does not show compassion and charity for these does not deserve to receive the same from God.
St. Vincent de Paul

St. Vincent was never surprised at any fault he saw committed, for, said he, it is proper to man to fall, since he was conceived and born in sin. This awareness he had of the common frailties of man caused him to treat all sinners compassionately and gently. He never employed sharp words, but rather kind ways and warm words.

✠

25. Among all those who come under the heading of *neighbor*, there is no one who deserves this name more than those with whom we live. These are the closest to us, living under the same roof and eating the same bread. Hence they must be among

the main recipients of our love. Toward them we must show true charity, which is not to be based on flesh and blood, or on their personal qualities, but solely on God. *St. Francis de Sales*

St. Jane Frances de Chantal had great charity toward her neighbor. But greater, more intense, and more tender was her love for her Sisters. Moreover, she sought to inculcate in them this love for one another. In order to impress this on them she pointed out in a conference: "Notice that when Jesus Christ imposed fraternal charity upon the Apostles, He said one thing about the love they should have for everyone and another about the love they were to have for each other. Speaking of the first, He said: 'Love your neighbor as yourself.' Of the second He exhorted: 'Love one another as I have loved you and as the Father loves Me.'"

☩

26. Sometimes God grants a certain union of heart and tender love toward one's neighbor, which is one of the greatest and most excellent gifts His divine goodness can give to man.
St. Francis de Sales

The same saint had received this beautiful gift. One day, while conversing with a friend of his, St. Francis confided: "I believe there is not another soul who loves more wholeheartedly, more tenderly and, if you can say it, 'more lovingly' than I, for it pleased God to form my heart this way."

✠

27. It is not enough to love our neighbor; we must see if we have the right kind of love. If we love our neighbor because he is good to us—he loves us and gives us help, honor or pleasure—this is a love known as concupiscence and we have it in common with animals. If we love someone because of something we see in him, that is, attractive appearance, manners, a leaning toward us, charm, etc., this is a love called friendship and we share it with pagans. Neither one of these loves is true love, but rather a love without value, because both are just natural loves, of short duration, being based on motives which often vanish. True love, which alone is meritorious and lasting, springs from charity, which leads us to love our neighbor in God and for God— that is, because this is pleasing to God, or because that person is dear to God, because God is in him or so that He may be in him. Oh, how true this love is! *St. Francis de Sales*

For this reason he had a great love and respect for everyone, seeing God in every soul and every soul in God. And for this reason, also, he was exceptionally courteous with all. He tenderly loved his friends, but because he loved them in God, he was always ready to deprive himself of their company. In writing to the superior of a Convent, he warned: "Keep the scale with your daughters straight, so that their natural gifts will not cause you to be partial in the distribution of your affections and of the various duties. How many people externally unattractive are very pleasing to God! Beauty, charm, pleasant speech, and gracious ways win favor with those who still live according to their inclinations. Charity looks for the real virtues, the beauty of the soul, and embraces everyone impartially."

☨

28. When shall we be steeped in tenderness and goodness toward our neighbor? When we view their souls in the Heart of Christ! Whoever looks upon his neighbor in any other light runs the risk of loving him neither purely, constantly, nor equally. In Christ's Heart, however, who would not love him? Who would not bear with him? Who would not put up with his imperfections? Who would find him annoying? Now, in fact, our neighbor is to be found on our Divine Savior's bosom.

St. Francis de Sales

This was the principal reason why the holy prelate was so affable, so amiable and so respectful toward everyone. He saw everyone in the Heart of Christ.

This also was one of St. Vincent de Paul's maxims. He did not consider a person's exterior alone, but as he was in God. He would say, "I must not look at the appearance and natural qualities of some poor fellow or old lady, because at times they barely appear to be rational creatures, so ill-mannered and rough are they. But if we

Charity

look at them with the light of faith, we find them engraved deep in the Heart of the Son of God, Who went to the point of giving His life for each one of them."

☖

29. When Raguel saw the young Tobias, whom he had never seen before, he exclaimed: "Oh! How much this youth resembles my cousin!" Upon hearing that he was his cousin's son, he embraced him tightly, and blessed him again and again, weeping over him lovingly. Why? Not because of his good qualities, because as yet he did not know him, but because, as he said, "You are the son of a very good person and you resemble him very much." Do you see what love does when it is true? If we really loved God, we would treat all our neighbors in like manner, for they are all children of God and resemble Him greatly. *St. Francis de Sales*

Frequently St. Mary Magdalene de Pazzi considered the image of God in her Sisters, which practice aroused in her a greater love for them. When she saw one apparently unrefined and imperfect, she would reflect that perhaps that Sister had some interior gift because of which God was pleased with her.

A holy Religious made this resolution: "I will love God for Himself, and for His love, I will serve His images. I will give my heart to Him, and my hands to my fellow men in order to unite them with Him."

✠

30-31. Of all the means of acquiring and preserving union with and love for God and neighbor, I have found nothing better or more efficacious than holy humility. Humility causes us to place ourselves below everyone, considering ourselves the least and the most unworthy of all. It keeps us from thinking evil of anyone. Self-love and pride, on the other hand, lead us to uphold our ideas against those of others, and thus the love we owe them grows cold. *St. Vincent de Paul*

In the course of a sermon, a Franciscan preacher strongly condemned a vice of which a certain Marquis, present in the Congregation, was guilty. After the sermon, the latter went up to the priest and heaped insults upon him. He then demanded, "Do you know who I am?" The Franciscan answered: "Yes, and I deem myself honored to know such a noble man, I who am a peasant by birth, and the least of men." Appeased by such an answer, the Marquis left with tears in his eyes and a sincere veneration for that priest.

DECEMBER

Union

> God is love, and he who abides in love abides in God, and God in him. 1 John 4:16.

1. The purpose of all virtue is to lead us to union with God, in which alone is to be found all the happiness possible in this world. Now, in what precisely does this union consist? In nothing else than the perfect conformity and similarity of our will with the will of God. These two wills are to be in complete conformity with one another, so that there is nothing in one which is repugnant to the other; whatever one desires and loves; whatever one likes or dislikes, the other likes or dislikes also.
St. John of the Cross

The Blessed Mother had this perfect union with God and, according to St. Bernard, she kept her gaze unceasingly on His divine will and was ever completely disposed to follow it.

✠

2. They deceive themselves who think that union with God consists of ecstasies and delights in Him. It consists of nothing else than the submission of our will, with our thoughts, words, and actions, to the will of God. Union is perfect when the will is

detached from everything and adheres totally to God in such a manner that its every movement is nothing else but the pure will of God. This is the true and essential union which I have always desired and unceasingly asked of God.

St. Teresa of Avila

St. Teresa never ceased to marvel over man's great fortune in being able to unite himself to His Creator, and over the tremendous yearning that God has to see us united to Him. This was the object of all her desires and that which she ardently sought above everything else.

St. John the Baptist lived in the desert for many years, despite his strong desire to join the company of our Savior. Attached to the will of God, he remained there doing his duty. Then, after beholding Him and baptizing Him, he did not follow Him, but continued doing his work. Oh, what is this if not detachment of the spirit from all things in order to do God's will? "This example," says St. Francis de Sales, "overwhelms me by its greatness."

✠

3. Union with God is accomplished in three ways: with conformity, uniformity and deiformity. Conformity is the total subordination of our will to the divine in all our actions, in every situation and event, desiring and accepting all that God wants and disposes, no matter how burdensome and repugnant this may be. Uniformity is a tight adhesion

of our will to the divine will by reason of which not only do we want it only because God wants it; hence we enjoy everything for the sole reason that the divine will finds pleasure in it and wants it. Deiformity is a transformation which makes our will one with the will of God, so that it no longer makes itself felt, as though it no longer existed, but rather feels only the divine will in itself.

Fr. Achille Gagliardi

St. Mary Magdalene de Pazzi attained to all three of these degrees of union with God. In regard to the third degree she lived without desires or will of her own. Such was the state of her soul which God let her see as someone else's during one of her ecstasies. She described that soul thus: "She followed her Spouse without understanding, without speaking, without hearing, without experiencing delight and, one might say, without acting, as one dead. She concentrated solely on following the divine Word in order not to offend Him."

✠

4. Conformity to the divine will is a very powerful means of overcoming any temptation, of correcting any imperfection, and of preserving peace of heart; it is a very efficacious remedy for all evils and the Christian's true treasure. It calls for a high degree of mortification, abnegation, holy indifference, imitation of Christ, union with God and in general all the virtues, which are virtues by the very

fact that they are conformed to the will of God, which is the origin and rule of all perfection.

St. Vincent de Paul

St. Vincent held this virtue so dearly that it may be called his principal and habitual virtue, the one which influenced all the others, and was the principal generator of all the powers of his soul, of all his sentiments, of all his exercises of piety, of all his holy practices and of all his actions. If he placed himself in the presence of God in prayer, he did it to say to God, as did St. Paul: "Lord, what do You want me to do?" If he was so careful to consult Our Lord and listen to Him, he did it to know the will of God with greater certainty and to dispose himself better to fulfill it. Finally, if he resolutely rejected the maxims of the world and attached himself solely to the teachings of the Gospels, it was all to conform more perfectly to the will of God.

☨

5. A soul who is really resigned to God's will does not become attached to any created thing because he sees clearly that all things are nothing except God. His one and only goal is to die to himself and to resign himself to God's will in all things always.

Blessed Henry Susone

St. Vincent de Paul was outstanding in this. He was completely detached from creatures and from himself, too. His sole concern was to be entirely submissive to the will of God and to the dispositions of His holy Providence.

✠

6. Since the Lord knows everyone, He permits for each what is most suitable to His own glory, the salvation of the individual soul, and the good of its neighbors. The mistake we make is not to entrust ourselves entirely to His will for us.
St. Teresa of Avila

Our Lord once gave St. Francis Borgia the power to choose between life and death for his beloved wife, who was seriously ill. Greatly moved, the Saint answered, "O Lord, why commit to my judgment what pertains to Your power alone? What matters to me is to fulfill Your holy will in everything, because no one more than You knows what is best for me."

✠

7. We must submit ourselves to the will of God and be content in whatever state of life or condition He is pleased to place us. Neither should we desire a change until we know it to be His will. This is the most excellent and the most profitable way of life.
St. Vincent de Paul

The Venerable Father Da Ponte confided to a friend that he rejoiced over his natural physical defects and defects of speech, because God had been pleased to mark him thus. Likewise, he rejoiced at the temptations and human miseries which he experienced, both internal and external, because God willed them. Furthermore, if it should be God's will for him to live a thousand years weighed down with even greater trials, he would be happy, as long as he did not offend Him.

When St. Elizabeth was told of her husband's death, she at once turned to the Lord and said, "You well know that I preferred his company to all the delights of the world. But since it has pleased You to take him from me, I accept Your will completely."

✠

8. Do not think you have attained to that degree of purification that is required until your will is entirely and in all things—even the most distasteful—freely and cheerfully submissive to the holy will of God. *St. Francis de Sales*

St. Jane Frances de Chantal tells us that St. Francis had himself reached such a degree of purification that even in the greatest of his afflictions he experienced inner consolation a hundred times sweeter than the ordinary—the result of his uninterrupted intimate union with God.

His Congregation having sustained a considerable loss, St. Vincent de Paul informed a friend of it in these words: "I must tell you of the loss we have suffered, yet I do not communicate it as an evil that has befallen us, but rather, as a favor God has granted us. I call the afflictions He sends us favors and blessings, especially when they are well received."

✠

9. One act of resignation to the divine will when its dispositions are contrary to our taste is worth more than a thousand successes achieved in accordance with our own desires and will.
St. Vincent de Paul

How much merit holy Job gained when he exclaimed amid his many sorrows: "The Lord has given, and the Lord has taken away"!

✠

10. Perfect resignation is nothing else than extreme annihilation of one's thoughts and affections, by which one gives himself entirely to God, so that in all things He may guide him as He pleases. It is as though the soul no longer knows or desires himself or anything else outside of God. Consequently he loses himself in God. *Blessed Henry Susone*

St. Catherine of Genoa was one of those fortunate souls who achieved this holy annihilation to the point where she no longer had any thoughts, affections or desires other than to leave everything up to God without any resistance or choice on her part. For this reason, she constantly experienced the joys of the Blessed, who have no other will than the will of their God. Hence, she used to say: "Whether I eat, drink, speak, keep silent, sleep or wake, see, hear, or think; whether I am in church, at home or on the street;

whether ill or healthy, in every hour and at every moment of my life I want everything to be in God and for God. In fact, I would like to be incapable of doing, saying or thinking anything other than what God wills."

✠

11. When will we experience the sweetness of the divine will in all that happens, paying no attention to anything but His good pleasure, which sends us adversity as well as prosperity, but with the same love and for our own good? When will we abandon ourselves completely to the embrace of our all-loving Heavenly Father, leaving it to Him to take care of us and our affairs, and reserving for ourselves only the desire to please Him and to serve Him as well as we can?   *St. Jane Frances de Chantal*

St. Jane Frances used to accept all occurrences—joyful and otherwise—with the same indifference. Her one desire was that God should do with her as He pleased.

✠

12. To abandon oneself to God simply consists in the total gift of our will to Him. When a soul can really say: "Lord, I have no other will but Yours," he has truly abandoned himself to God and is united to Him.   *St. Francis de Sales*

Union

One day Our Lord appeared to St. Gertrude and said: "Behold, My daughter, in one hand I hold health, and in the other, illness. Choose the one you prefer." Throwing herself at His feet the saint cried: "Lord, I beg You not to give any thought to my will, only Yours. Do with me as You wish." Our Lord was very pleased with this answer and added: "Let those who wish Me to visit them often give Me the key to their will and never ask for it back."

✠

13. Many souls tell Our Lord: "I give myself entirely to You without reserve," but few really practice this abandonment. For it consists of a kind of indifference to whatever happens in accordance with the plans of divine Providence—afflictions as well as consolations, contempt and disdain as well as honor and glory. *St. Francis de Sales*

Outstanding in this regard was St. Vincent de Paul. Always and everywhere, in all his duties, in every occasion, in tribulations or consolations, in sickness, in scorching heat or biting cold, when insulted, calumniated, or reproved, in times of bereavement, in material losses—never did St. Vincent become upset or disturbed. For him it was as if one event were the same as another: he never lost his deep peace of soul. This peace was in fact evident in his gentle words and serene countenance.

✠

14. If you throw yourself wholeheartedly into the practice of holy abandonment, without hardly noticing it you will make much progress, just as do the passengers on board a ship sailing on the high sea under favorable winds, relying completely on the guidance of the captain.   *St. Francis de Sales*

A certain religious had become famous as a miracle-worker. The sick were cured by simply touching his clothes. His Abbot was greatly amazed, for he could see nothing special about him. One day he asked the religious why God was working such miracles through him. "I do not know," came the reply, "because I do not fast, scourge myself, stay up nights, exhaust myself working, pray for long hours, or do anything else out of the ordinary. The only thing I do is this: no matter what happens, I do not let myself become upset or disturbed. I retain peace of soul even in afflictions, because I leave everything to God. Success or difficulty, abundance or want—I accept it all from Him with equal gratitude."

"This, then, is the reason for your miracles," concluded the Abbot.

✠

15. One of the chief effects of holy abandonment in God is an unchanging spirit through the ups and downs of this life.   *St. Francis de Sales*

Taulero tells us that for eight years a well-known theologian had been praying for the grace to find someone to teach him the way of truth. Finally, one day, while renewing this petition with even more fervor than usual he had the following inspiration: "Go to the church and there you will find him." He obeyed but encountered no one except a poor beggar on the church steps. The poor man was pitifully wrapped in soiled garments and his body was covered with sores. Moved to compassion, the theologian greeted him kindly: "May God give you a good day, sir."

"I have never had a bad one," replied the beggar cheerfully. "Well," said the theologian, "may God grant you good fortune, then." "I have never experienced misfortune," came the answer. "What?" exclaimed the theologian. "You have never had bad days and never experienced misfortune? Why, you are weighed down with sickness and poverty!"

To that the beggar said: "I have surrendered myself entirely to the divine will, to which I completely conform my own will. Hence whatever God wants, I want. When hunger, thirst, cold, heat and sickness afflict me, I do nothing but praise God. In both fair and foul weather, I praise Him."

"Tell me, where did you acquire such perfection?" "Through recollection, meditation and union with God. I was never able to find peace in anything less than God. Since I have found Him, I have enjoyed continual peace."

"And where did you find God?" "Where I left all affection for everything else."

☩

16. It is from this holy abandonment that the marvelous freedom of spirit enjoyed by the perfect comes. It is in this same surrender that all the hap-

piness desirable in this life is to be found, for when nothing is feared or longed for anymore, all things are had. *St. Teresa of Avila*

One such admirable soul was St. Francis de Sales. He always looked contented, as though everything were going his way. Indeed, when there arose fierce opposition to him and to the Order he had founded, he wrote to St. Jane Frances de Chantal: "I leave all these trials up to Divine Providence. They can continue or cease, as it pleases God. I am as content with the storm as with the calm. If the world did not criticize us, we would not be servants of God."

☧

17. How wonderful it is to see someone devoid of all attachments, ready to perform any act of virtue and charity, amiable with all, willing to undertake any labor, unchanging in consolations and tribulations alike, and completely happy as long as the will of God is being done! *St. Francis de Sales*

This was a description of himself, as is clear from many examples given elsewhere in this book.

☧

18. When we shall have surrendered completely to the will of God, submitting our will and all our affections without reserve to His rule, we shall see our souls totally united to God. *St. Francis de Sales*

Union

Those who knew St. Francis more intimately in his last years attest that he reached the point where he neither willed, loved, nor saw anything but God in all things. He was always absorbed in God and would declare that nothing in the world could make him happy—only God. Very often he would exclaim: "O Lord, what is there in heaven or what could I desire on earth except You? You are my portion and my heredity forever."

✠

19. When one wants to be united to God, he must examine himself to see if there is some obstacle between his soul and God and if he seeks himself in anything or directs anything toward himself.
Blessed Henry Susone

A famous cavalier who had lived at court a good part of his life, conforming to the ways of the world, was finally won over to God by St. Vincent de Paul. He began at once to strive so hard for self-perfection that he was of great example to all. Desirous of progressing steadily and convinced that only to the degree that he detached himself from creatures would he be united to God, he frequently examined himself to see if he were still attached to relatives, friends, possessions, honors, comforts or anything else. Whatever he discovered to be holding him back he would cut off. One day, while on horseback, he began to examine himself as usual. Realizing clearly that he was deeply attached to his sword, which had served him so faithfully in many a duel, he dismounted and broke it in two on a rock. When relating this fact to St. Vincent, the cavalier declared: "I experienced such a great freedom afterwards that never again did I feel an attachment to anything."

✠

20. The effort to attain to union with God consists simply in striving to die totally to everything worldly and attending to the enjoyment of God.
St. Teresa of Avila

St. Catherine of Genoa lived in this blessed state. She confessed that once she had a vision in which she was shown how all good comes from the goodness of God. "At this," she said, "such a love was born in me that from that moment on, I lost all thought, desire and love for anything but God."

✠

21. No matter how much virtue a soul may have, if his heart is attached to something, even a trifle, he will never attain to the freedom of divine union. If a bird is tied down with a fine thread, despite the fineness of the thread, the bird is still bound. How greatly to be pitied are certain souls rich in good works, virtues and favors from God yet lacking in the courage to break off a little attachment or to give up a certain satisfaction. As a result, they can never arrive at union with God which consists in snapping that thread and soaring into flight! Once the soul is free from every affection for creatures, God cannot do else but communicate

Himself to her fully, just as the sun on a clear day cannot help but brighten an open room.

St. John Chrysostom

We read in the life of St. Gregory that a very wealthy man left the world and retired to a forest. Of all his possessions he took nothing but his kitten as a little comfort in his solitude. Therefore, he loved the kitten and often patted it. After living for many years in continual prayer and penance, he asked Our Lord to let him know what reward awaited him. Our Lord gave him to understand that he could receive a reward in heaven equal to St. Gregory's. The good man was saddened by this answer. He could not see why one who had left all he had to serve God with such an austere way of life should receive no greater reward than one who had lived amid great wealth and comfort. But God enlightened him and made it plain to him that he was more attached to his cat than Gregory was to all the riches and honors he enjoyed and, furthermore, that perfection consists in detachment from everything.

✠

22. The reason we never reach sanctity, despite the many communions we receive, is that we do not let God reign in us as He yearns. He comes to us and finds our hearts full of desires, affections and little vanities. This is not what He wants. He would like to find them completely empty so that He could rule as the absolute Sovereign there.

St. Francis de Sales

St. Louis Gonzaga would center his whole week around the reception of Holy Communion. In preparation he offered all his actions of the three days preceding and, in thanksgiving, those of the last three days.

☩

23. To attain to perfect union with God, perfect, total mortification of the senses and the appetites is strictly required. The best and the shortest way to achieve this mortification of the senses is to reject at once whatever pleasure offers itself that is not purely for the glory of God, and to do this for love of Jesus Christ, Who never took any pleasure or wanted any in this world except the joy of doing His Father's Will. *St. John of the Cross*

Such, precisely, was the life of this Saint: an uninterrupted practice of internal and external mortification, which he never considered enough. Hence he achieved a great union with God.

St. Francis Borgia frequently begged Our Lord to make all the comforts of life distasteful to him and he himself did his best to make them so. He greatly desired, attentively sought and happily embraced all that was disagreeable to self-love with regard to food, dress, and home. By so doing, he greatly progressed in virtue and holy union.

✠

24. If you ardently desire union with God, let your way of life be as interior as possible. Do not be such an extrovert as to reveal yourself by word or gesture or action. Try to be recollected within yourself and attentive to God alone, Who is present to you. Exclude from your heart all that you see and hear. *Blessed Henry Susone*

At one time Father Alvarez was noticed to be deep in thought for a number of days. When asked what was wrong, he replied: "I am trying to determine a way of living as though I were in the wilds of Africa and of keeping my heart as detached from creatures as though I really were in the wilderness."

✠

25. Be resolved to remain in the presence of God by means of a complete divesting of self and surrender to His holy will. Each time you find your spirit straying from this precious company, bring it back gently. This love consisting of simple confidence and the repose of the spirit on the Paternal bosom of Divine Goodness contains all that one could desire to please God. *St. Francis de Sales*

This was one of St. Jane Frances de Chantal's most treasured and most frequent practices. She did it by simply turning to God and adhering to His will, reposing in it like a child in his mother's arms. She made no attempt to do anything else or to find out what God was working in her.

☩

26. When I see certain souls very diligent and attentive in prayer, their heads bowed, evidently afraid to move even the slightest bit or let their thoughts waver for a moment lest they lose anything of the sensible delight and devotion they have experienced, I realize how little they understand the way to achieve union. They think that their whole care must be to concentrate on nothing but this. No, no! God wants deeds. When you are given something to do for obedience or charity towards your neighbor, do not worry about losing that devotion, that thought and enjoyment of God. Giving Him pleasure by doing these other things will lead you much faster to that holy union.   *St. Teresa of Avila*

When St. Mary Magdalene de Pazzi was a novice, she sometimes had her Novice Mistress' permission to retire to pray while her companions performed various types of manual labor. She, however, never took advantage of these permissions, declaring that she preferred to be busy about some work in obedience, even if menial and tiring, than in even the highest level of contemplation. When asked why, she replied: "Because by performing the duties of religious life and obedience, I am sure of doing the will of God, while I am not sure of doing so when I pray or do some other work, no matter how good and holy, but of my own choosing."

☩

27. Our own will, as God tells us through His Prophet, is what spoils and corrupts all our devotions, labors and penances. Hence, not to waste time and energy, we must see to it that we never act out of natural reasons, self-interests, our own inclinations, moods, or whims, but always solely to carry out the will of God. We must become accustomed to doing so in all things, for it is the way, the only way, in fact, to reach divine union quickly and surely. *St. Vincent de Paul*

It was St. Vincent de Paul's sole concern not to undertake anything to which he was not clearly directed by the will of God. His humility always made him distrust the inspirations he personally received and fear self-deception.

St. Catherine of Genoa well understood the importance of doing God's will in order to attain to divine union. She once said, "There is no greater disease than self-will. It is so subtle and innate, it hides itself in so many ways and defends itself with so many arguments that it seems a real devil. When it cannot reach its goal one way, it finds another under various pretexts, such as for sanctity, necessity, charity, justice, or to suffer for God, to enjoy some spiritual consolation, to give good example, to condescend to others. I see in this self-will an abyss of malice, so ruinous and so opposed to God that only He can free us from it."

✠

28. To attain to divine union, all the troubles God sends us are required. By means of these, He wipes out all our lower inclinations. Hence, all the insults, injuries, contempt, infirmities, abandonment by relatives and friends, embarrassments, temptations of the devil and other events distasteful to our human nature—all are extremely necessary so that we will fight until we have extinguished our evil inclinations. Until our troubles no longer seem bitter but rather, sweet for love of God, we will never reach divine union.

St. Catherine of Genoa

"That this is so," says the same Saint, "I know by experience. When Divine Love sees how tightly we cling to what we have chosen to love, because to us it appears beautiful, good and right, and blinded by our self-love, we will not hear a word to the contrary, He takes away everything to which we have given our heart. Hence we reach the point of not knowing what to do with ourselves, since we have been torn from those things in which we took delight and are experiencing only suffering and confusion. And not knowing why God permits these things, which seem unreasonable, we become irritated and go about moaning and trying our best to find relief from so much anxiety. When Divine Love has kept the soul in this state of suspense for some time, almost despairing and now annoyed by all that it formerly loved, He suddenly reveals Himself, His divine countenance resplendant and lovable to behold."

St. Elizabeth, daughter of the King of Hungary, was widowed while still young. Her property and money were taken from her, she was put out of her own home, abandoned by everyone and made to suffer from slander, affronts and insults. All this she suffered very patiently for the love of God. He in turn amply rewarded her for everything with wondrous spiritual gifts.

✠

29. To acquire perfection in general and all the virtues in particular to the point of attaining union with God, we need to keep a model before our eyes to serve as our guiding rule in all actions and attempts to progress. Now, beyond any doubt, no more perfect or surer exemplar could we take than the one God Himself gave us in the person of His divine Son. Blessed is he who imitates Him best!
St. Vincent de Paul

The habitual, constant practice of this saint was precisely that of governing himself in all his affairs according to the examples and teachings of our Savior, which he ever kept before his eyes so as to imitate Him in everything. Every time he had to make a decision, give advice or make some recommendation, he would at once consult the life and teachings of Christ for confirmation of his view. Seldom did he speak without mentioning something about the Son of God or referring to one of His teachings. His applications of them, moreover, were so apt that they made a great impression on his hearers. And when nothing regarding a particular matter came to his mind, he would say to himself, "What would Christ say, what would He do in this situation?" Then he would take the course of action it seemed to him Christ would have taken.

✠

30-31. Oh, what remorse we will have at the end of our lives on considering the great number of examples given us by God and the saints for our perfection—examples so neglected by us! If today marked the end of your life, would you be satisfied with the way you have lived this year?

St. Francis de Sales

Thomas a Kempis relates that a pious soul once became greatly upset and worried about his final perseverance. Prostrating himself before the altar, he prayed: "Oh, if I only knew that I would persevere in good will to the end!" At that he heard an interior voice replying: "And if you knew it, what would you do? Do now what you will wish to have done at the end of your life, and you will feel secure."

It is related in the lives of the Fathers that once when an elderly monk was asked what he had done to acquire perfection, he replied, "The moment I left the world I said to myself: 'Today you have been born again; today you are beginning to serve God and to live in this holy place. Daily begin life anew as though the next day were to be your last.' This is exactly what I have done every day."

St. Paul Book & Media Centers

ALASKA
750 West 5th Ave., Anchorage, AK 99501 907-272-8183.

CALIFORNIA
3908 Sepulveda Blvd., Culver City, CA 90230 310-397-8676.
1570 Fifth Ave. (at Cedar Street), San Diego, CA 92101 619-232-1442; 619-232-1443.
46 Geary Street, San Francisco, CA 94108 415-781-5180.

FLORIDA
145 S.W. 107th Ave., Miami, FL 33174 305-559-6715; 305-559-6716.

HAWAII
1143 Bishop Street, Honolulu, HI 96813 808-521-2731.

ILLINOIS
172 North Michigan Ave., Chicago, IL 60601 312-346-4228; 312-346-3240.

LOUISIANA
4403 Veterans Memorial Blvd., Metairie, LA 70006 504-887-7631; 504-887-0113.

MASSACHUSETTS
50 St. Paul's Ave., Jamaica Plain, Boston, MA 02130 617-522-8911.
Rte. 1, 885 Providence Hwy., Dedham, MA 02026 617-326-5385.

MISSOURI
9804 Watson Rd., St. Louis, MO 63126 314-965-3512; 314-965-3571.

NEW JERSEY
561 U.S. Route 1, Wick Plaza, Edison, NJ 08817 908-572-1200.

NEW YORK
150 East 52nd Street, New York, NY 10022 212-754-1110.
78 Fort Place, Staten Island, NY 10301 718-447-5071; 718-447-5086.

OHIO
2105 Ontario Street (at Prospect Ave.), Cleveland, OH 44115 216-621-9427.

PENNSYLVANIA
214 W. DeKalb Pike, King of Prussia, PA 19406 215-337-1882; 215-337-2077.

SOUTH CAROLINA
243 King Street, Charleston, SC 29401 803-577-0175.

TEXAS
114 Main Plaza, San Antonio, TX 78205 210-224-8101.

VIRGINIA
1025 King Street, Alexandria, VA 22314 703-549-3806.

CANADA
3022 Dufferin Street, Toronto, Ontario, Canada M6B 3T5 416-781-9131.